CONTACT WITH THE DEPTHS

CONTACT WITH THE DEPTHS

Michael Eigen

KARNAC

First published in 2011 by
Karnac Books Ltd
118 Finchley Road, London NW3 5HT

British Library Cataloguing in Publication Data

A C.I.P. for this book is available from the British Library

   ISBN: 978 1 85575 847 6

Edited, designed and produced by The Studio Publishing Services Ltd
www.publishingservicesuk.co.uk
e-mail: studio@publishingservicesuk.co.uk

Printed and bound in Great Britain by Berforts Information Press Ltd.

www.karnacbooks.com

CONTENTS

ABOUT THE AUTHOR

Michael Eigen has been practising in the mental health field for over fifty years, first with disturbed children in schools and treatment centres, then as a psychoanalytic psychotherapist, psychoanalyst, and psychologist in clinic and individual practice. He has taught at several universities, including the New York University Postdoctoral Program in Psychotherapy and Psychoanalysis. He has also taught at many psychoanalytic institutes, including directing a programme for creative individuals in psychoanalysis. He was Director of Training at the Institute for Expressive Analysis and is currently on the faculty as a control/training analyst of the National Psychological Association for Psychoanalysis, where he was on the Board of Directors for eight years. He has published over one hundred papers and eighteen books.

Introduction and acknowledgements

"Distinction–union structure", Chapter One, was written in response to an invitation by Dr Alan Barnett to contribute to a special issue on creativity in psychoanalysis for *Psychoanalytic Inquiry*. In *The Psychotic Core* and elsewhere (*The Electrified Tightrope, Coming Through the Whirlwind, Reshaping the Self*), I posited a distinction–union structure as a kind of DNA/RNA of psychic life. Every moment is made up of distinction and union tendencies. While distinction and union may have their own biographies and trajectories, they are co-present in each psychic event. Dr Barnett felt it would be useful to say more about this structure or co-reality, and I have tried to do so here.

I trace the play of distinction–union tendencies in cases I have worked with and in a number of cultural phenomena. It is important to point out that I am positing distinction–union as an elemental structure made up of co-tendencies. A kind of double directionality, dual tendencies, parts of a more basic structure, structure within structure. Structure, too, is another name for process. I do not distinguish between structure and process. Structures are the work of processes which spontaneously order themselves. We are made of structural processes.

"Spirituality and addiction" (Chapter Two) grew from a talk I gave for the Psychoanalytic Psychotherapy Study Center in 2008, a meeting developed by The Committee on Psychoanalysis and Addictions Treatment. In this study, I relate addiction to wounded aloneness in infancy. Winnicott writes of a "primary aloneness" that must be supported by the care-taker, although the infant may not be aware of this support. In part, I describe this as aloneness supported by an unknown, boundless other (2009, Chapters One and Two).

Addiction tries to heal the wound to this aloneness or call attention to this wound. In Chapter Two, I trace variations of wounded aloneness and its relation to addiction in several cases. Through the forms of interaction therapy sessions create, the qualities of aloneness and connection of therapist and patient deepen and evolve. Three addictions described here involve alcoholism, drugs, and medication. Faith or its lack plays an important role in the patient and therapist managing to get through sessions and letting something more happen.

"I don't know" (Chapter Three) was given as a seminar on Buddhism and Psychoanalysis at the American Psychoanalytic Association meeting in 2009. These three words are often denigrated. In political life, one tries to appear to know. Yet, grave dangers result from pretence of knowledge, miscalculation from the viewpoint of thinking one knows something one does not. The delusion that Iraq threatened us with weapons of mass destruction is one such psychopathic estimate. Daily life is filled with them. There is pressure to act as if one knows and shame attached to not knowing.

What a relief to feel and say and hear, "I don't know". Chapter Three elaborates on the theme of not knowing as experience and methodology. It traces benefits of not knowing in psychoanalysis, spiritual and cultural life. Much needless pressure to be or act like we are not would find some relief if these three little words, "I don't know", were assimilated into political and personal existence.

"Wordlessness" (Chapter Four) was given as a talk for the International Forum of Psychoanalytic Education in 2009, the Hans Loewald Award presentation. It brings out the importance of wordless depths in our lives, in art, problem solving, ethical feeling, spiritual experience, emotional contact, and processing. Poetry often uses words to thrill us with wordless depths. Mystical experience lives in wordless mystery, often pointed to by words. It is as if we live in a wordless emotive ocean that we access a little at a time. The quality of links between words and wordlessness makes a difference in the quality of our existence.

"Ring–hang up, stop–start, on–off" (Chapter Five) grew out of my Bion seminar, now ongoing over thirty years. Aspects of this chapter were presented in seminars in Seattle, San Francisco, Tel Aviv, and Seoul. The chapter begins with three incidents in my practice involving phone mishaps, where miscommunication was part of the communication process and, in the third case, was not a miss at all. Two of the cases involved ringing and hanging up the phone as soon as it was picked up.

I relate ring–hang up communication to larger start–stop processes. It is not unusual for experience and behaviour to move in starts and stops. Approach–avoidance behaviour is one example. One moves towards someone then away, often needing a break from contact that might build. For some, this happens with work projects, making completion of tasks difficult.

To bring out aspects of this pattern, I use a Bion case in which an individual incessantly starts–stops the build-up of contact. It is as if making contact is precisely through a start–stop pattern. Bion writes of his frustration, feeling nothing builds in sessions, then reflects that this very frustration may be part of the patient's emotional communication.

I relate start–stop experiencing and communicating to a broader mode of on–off experiencing. Bion notes that one moment a dream is there, then it is gone. Now we see things one way, now another. This can apply to the rise and fall of self-feeling, now self, now no-self. On–off experience can be frustrating, even terrifying, but also a part of creativity, part of how processing ability works.

"Tears of pain and beauty: mixed voices" (Chapter Six) depicts a man's journey from a life beset with psychotic breakdowns to a long-term productive existence, medication and hospital free. We trace his move from isolation and fear, at first in baby steps, making contact with aspects of the world that he gravitates towards. In time, his contact expands and deepens, filtered through a sense of something basic, *simpatico* with his bent and disposition. An important part of this man's path was his intensity of experiencing. He was drawn to things that moved him and the appreciation and wonder this evoked made a difference. Contact with beauty was important to him. The beauty of nature at the beginning of recovery, but, as he became more at ease, lines and energy of cities, faces, souls, spirits, often in the most humble places and people.

"Arm falling off" (Chapter Seven) explores a patient's dream reported by Bion, in which the patient tries to avert a feared disaster, losing an arm in the process. One disaster supplants another. Bion calls attention to myths emphasizing the turn of something good to something bad, for example, The Garden of Eden, the Tower of Babel. Such a sequence is ubiquitous in silent films, which, comically, hit deep, poignant nerves.

Examples from spiritual writings and my own clinical practice are used to highlight twists and turns of the "fall", the "disturbance", the thing that goes wrong. Partly to acknowledge it, not justify it, but also to note what this tendency accomplishes, for it does good as well as evil. Why are we so destructive? What does destructiveness accomplish? Why are we so attached to it? What does it do for us? Does destructiveness, in some way, stimulate greater intensity of experience, intense concentration? This chapter is not exhaustive, but suggestive. It brings out a field of experience requiring attention and care.

"Music and psychoanalysis" (Chapter Eight) was originally published as "Interview with Michael Eigen (carried out by e-mail with Stephen Bloch as the principal interviewer)" for a book co-edited by Paul W. Ashton and Stephen Bloch, *Psyche and Music: Contemporary Psychoanalytic Explorations* (Spring Journal Books, 2010).

The ancients wrote about the music of the spheres. There is also music of the psyche. We feel the pulse of sessions, currents, sub-currents, flows, and blocks. Freud wrote of something wrong in the rhythm of the psyche. Work in sessions is, to an important degree, an improvisational art. Bion spoke of a difference between cacophony and music, the latter related to psychic nourishment. The music of a life, a session, a psyche related to discord, harmony, dissonance, resolution, upheaval, pathos, grief, sublime thrills beyond words. I am grateful for the chance Drs Bloch and Ashton gave me to explore my personal relationship to music and especially musical aspects of our work.

Taken together, the chapters of this book touch on different facets of contact with the depths, contact and loss or break of contact, and failure of contact to be born. There are many qualities of contact with life, who we are and what our lives feel like. Contact and jeopardy to contact, deformations of contact. As a human group we are in the midst of a great journey, exploring ways we make contact with reality, contact with subjectivity, ways we constitute reality and reality constitutes us. It is awesome to be a living being who feels, cries, laughs, sings, dies. Who hurts others and is hurt, who goes mad, becomes inspired, or is just happy to be alive to each day to the extent one can. Life never ceases being an unpredictable sea, raising up, dashing down, pressing us through ranges of emotions, more alive, threatened, empty, deadened, eager. Bion wrote that his ability to make and sustain contact was challenged. I think he was being honest, telling it as it is. Our contact with life, ourselves, each other *is* challenged. And through it all, we have need for deep contact, contact with the depths, fulfilling and suspenseful. Contact we never stop growing into, a challenge daily growing in importance.

And what of surface–depth connection? So many possibilities of connection–disconnection. We are sensitive to new structures, emergence of capacities, discontinuity, evolution, gaps between dimensions, splits between affective attitudes, divisions. Yet, there is also a fit between surface–depth. A moment of beauty makes us quiver through and though, reverberates through our being, touches foundations, an experience that ripples through sensation, feeling, thinking, action, ethics (*Feeling Matters*, Chapter One). At that moment the gap is bridged, suspended (not obliterated). Connection between outside–inside and inner layering permeates us and we realize how interlaced we are with what, at other times, may seem remote. Consciousness not only separates, it brings together, it turns possibilities around, interlocks, fuses. As Chapter One distils, tendencies to distinguish and unite work together.

The chapters that follow touch ways we link up with our capacities, partner and struggle with them, benefit and harm ourselves by necessary trial and error. We see how interfusion of surface and depth characterizes the movement from psychosis to fuller life, in which sensitivity grows to encompass new levels, rather than is lost (Chapters Two, Six). We see how freeing "I don't know" (Chapter Three) and "wordlessness" (Chapters Four, Eight) can be and sense their linking presence in daily life. At the same time, we work with a need to break connections, start again, undo what we build, as if our creations make us claustrophobic, as if we feel hemmed in by what we produce (Chapters Five, Seven). Our mixed capacities can stymie us, cause confusion, a kind of centipede not knowing how to use its legs. But they also are a source of plasticity, ability to survive and survive well—if only we keep learning how to use our evolving makeup, do not give up on it, or it on us.

"Whatever happens opens reality."

Michael Eigen

"One never recovers from being human."

Michael Eigen

"Its exquisite peal permeates everywhere."

Dogen

". . . of trust and trembling fears,
a spark, as in the beginning."

Merle Molofsky

CHAPTER ONE

Distinction–union structure

Over twenty years ago (1986, Chapter Four; see also 1992, 1993, 1995) I posited a distinction–union structure as a kind of DNA–RNA of experience. Every micro-moment or "cell" of experience is made of distinction–union tendencies. More, that distinction–union tendencies are parts of one structure or event, always mixed and working, although either may be more dominant or obvious at any moment.

It might help living one's way into this by supposing distinction–union tendencies as branches of a single trunk, or roots in a complex root system. At some unobservable level, my hunch is that they are one, indistinguishable, but our representational cognitive language discriminates coincidence as two or more, often as binaries, opposites or complements.

What would it mean to posit them as indistinguishable and unobservable? Would this mean they are beyond knowing? I suspect there are vast "domains" we do not, and possibly cannot, know, yet they work and influence us, even structure us. Bion's (1965, 1970; Eigen, 1998) nameless, wordless Transformations in O point to this, as do countless wordless Buddha-lands beyond conscious categories pointed to in many sutras (e.g., Goddard, 1932, p. 46).

This chapter dips in and out of mystery, is steeped in it, but, for the most part, tries to attend to more or less expressible depictions of tendencies that come into view in inner vision and thought, tendencies that have had a long cultural history and strong psychoanalytic presence as well.

Cultural background

The triune doctrine of the Holy Trinity is a dramatic example of a distinction–union structure. God the Father, the Son, and the Holy Spirit are one-yet-three. There was disagreement among Catholic thinkers as to whether the Father and Son were one or two "substances". The Council of Nicaea in 325 CE settled on one "substance" yet three Persons. One-yet-distinct.

Critics might say such a reality or formulation is not understandable or beyond knowing. But one can venture a modern analogy by depicting different functions (respiration, digestion, circulation, etc.) of one body. The trope of one body to depict mystical connection or union between all people (even all life) has a long history. Saint Paul taught that all Christians were united as parts of Jesus' body. Jesus is credited with saying when two people commune in his name, he is there: three-yet-one in communion.

The "Sh'ma Yisroel" of Judaism has a many-in-one or one-in-many structure. It is often loosely translated as "Hear O Israel, the Lord our God, the Lord is One". This translation misses the fact that three names of God are used or implied in the famous dictum (or invitation): Sh'ma (hear, listen), Yisroel (Israel), Adonay (Lord, a substitute for the unsayable Ya-veh) Elokenu (God the many, many gods, plurality), Adonay (Lord, Lord God) echad (one). That is, God the many is one God. Ya is a name of God often meaning God Almighty (the one) in everyday talk, as in Hallelujah: Hallel (praise)—ya or ja (God).

It is hard to open an ancient text without finding some reference to the one-in-many. The *Bhagavad Gita*, for example: Krishna as all there is, one that is not only in but *is* all plurality. Here, the many-one are indistinguishable.

The way we so often think of or experience time is triune, past–present–future, three-yet-one. We speak of a stream of time, a flow, using liquid as a trope for a sense of duration, movement, enduring, an implicit sense of going on being. In inner reality, we experience ebbs and flows of time, heart time, pulse time, hunger time, breathing time. Our body is a mysterious field of experience that provides psychic time with many currents.

A modern physicist, David Bohm (1996), writes of implicate–explicate orders. Explicate refers to experiencing and thinking difference, the distinctness of beings, discriminated reality. Implicate points to unseen (unobservable?) connections, implicit oneness of reality where differentiation does not reign. The "wholeness" of the implicate order connects with Matte-Blanco's "symmetrical unconscious" and Bion's "transformations in O", which I will turn to in a moment. For now, I want to point out that a modern physicist created his own translation or amplification of the one-yet-many structure and saw it in ways the universe works. For Bohm (2004), the implicate order, by its unknown creative nature, gives rise to our own creative sense in work and life. We are expressions of creative processes that permeate the universe.

Psychoanalysis

The above cultural sampling has counterparts in psychoanalytic thinking, which we now dip into briefly. Matte-Blanco (1975, 1988) writes of a symmetrical unconscious and asymmetrical consciousness. As his work unfolds, he comes to mean two modes of being and thinking that permeate psychic life.

An example of symmetrical experiencing is the equality or identity of members of a set. All mothers in the set of mothers are identical in being women (symmetrical thinking), whatever their individual differences (asymmetrical thinking). By a spread of symmetrical thinking, awareness that all mothers are women can come to mean all women are mothers: that is, all women are seen as mothers. Symmetrical spreads characterize emotional contagion, where members of a set or across sets are reduced to characteristics that define the sets. Such melding can be part of the basis of prejudice but also a basis for mystical experience (e.g., all individuals in the set of humanity are alike in being human beings; therefore (in symmetrical spread), all people are one).

Symmetrical experiencing tends towards infinity, where anything can be anything else or nothing or everything. Asymmetrical experiencing puts the brakes on, emphasizing distinctions, individual differences, not-one. Of course, the differentiation tendency can proliferate, go haywire (as in infinite splitting), and we get into difficulties that parallel the identity tendency. Matte-Blanco describes many ways these two tendencies—movements towards identity or oneness and movements towards distinctness—are expressed in every psychic act. How to work with complex tendencies that add to existence is a perennial task, never more important than now.

Bion (1994) writes about fusion and splitting tendencies as simultaneous, oscillating, or alternate ways of organizing experience. At the deepest levels, they are indistinguishable, coincide (akin to Matte-Blanco's symmetrical). They are discriminated on a phenomenological level as perceived, conceptualized, or imagined tendencies. Something approaching a kind of indistinguishable "oneness" is seen in Bion's last words of *A Memoir of the Future* (1991, p. 578): "Wishing you all a Happy Lunacy and Relativistic Fission". Fission here combines splitting and fusion, as in the splitting of the atom in such a way that an earthly holocaust is feared: all as one tending towards zero.

Bion takes us still deeper when he speaks of K-transformations and O-transformations. K stands for knowledge, or knowing, and O for unknowable ultimate reality. He gives Freud as an example of rigid K transformations and Klein as an example of more fluid ones. Transformations in O remain a mystery approachable by F (faith, the psychoanalytic attitude). K transformations involve logic, narrative, words or mixtures of words and affects, numbers, drama. Transformations in O are wordless, imageless, ineffable. K can feed O and O can feed K, but O remains unknown and unknowable, although we try to learn about approaches to living O and ways of representing it.

For Bion, akin to Matte-Blanco, O is infinite: "The fundamental reality is 'infinity', the unknown, the situation for which there is no language" (Bion, 1994, p. 372). Nevertheless, we cannot exactly call O one or say it is not-one. Milner (1987) refers to it as 0 (zero). A lot goes on in O or 0. Transformations in O may be inscrutable and ineffable, but they matter. They contribute deeply to what we call growth. Transformations in O may be unobservable and inconceivable, but they are lived and contribute to living (James Grotstein has written deeply and imaginatively on O-processes and a primary subject–object of identification allied to distinction–union structures, e.g., 2000, 2007).

On the negative side, Bion posits a destructive force that goes on working after it destroys everything (1965, p. 101; Eigen, 1998, Chapter 3). How can destruction keep destroying after everything is destroyed? Much goes on in zero land.

Bion suggests we meet absolute destruction with Faith (F in O), faith in face of ultimate reality, an attitude of absolute openness (as open as one can be). Sometimes, when meditating on the faith that meets total destruction that goes on destroying, I think of Job: "Yea though You slay me, yet will I trust You". Job and Bion's F in O share a common core.

Bion calls F in O the psychoanalytic attitude and describes it as being without memory, desire, understanding, or expectation. A kind of zero or radical openness, letting go of self and mind-operations that maintain the latter, freedom from self and mind, a waiting on O. K formulations result and can prove important, but waiting on O, and not prematurely closing it off with K, can open transformational possibilities that may not happen without F. Part of waiting on O in F can be at-onement with oneself or, simply, atonement, with or without self.

What goes on in O we do not know, but we sense impacts, hints, intimations, some kind of contact with the unknown, although we cannot say what it is or is not. As a physicist once said, perhaps Eddington, something unknown is doing we do not know what. Its impacts affect us and we work with what we can. We, too, are that unknown or part of it. We are the unknown responding to itself.

Many psychoanalytic writers have views of how distinction–union develop and I have written about several of them in *The Psychotic Core* (1986, Chapter Four). Notions such as identification, primary, secondary and tertiary processes, projective identification, symbiosis–individuation, dual track, conjunction–disjunction, transitional space, use of object and primary aloneness are some of the important ones. More can be added. All share a sense that distinction–union tendencies are basic movements in experience and we read them in forces of nature as well.

Often distinction–union tendencies work unconsciously and become semi-visible in unexpected ways. I think of an early case near the beginning of my practice. I will call him Abe.[1] He was a serious alcoholic, binging to the point of waking up on the street after three or four days that were blank and never fully remembered. This was chronic, intermittent, reliable behaviour. He was in Alcoholics Anonymous, which helped, but he needed something else as well.

When he was sober for periods, his friends cheered him on. Inevitably, the fall would come and his friends tried to pick him up, expressed sadness, anger, disappointment, held out helping hands, encouraged him to come back and start again. But downspins came, as if blackout periods were needed, part of overarching up–down movements.

I, too, felt something like a Greek chorus, happy when he was all right, sad and scared when he dropped down. Happy–sad– scared was an implicit part of the therapy atmosphere. Through it, I tried to keep something of an even keel. Unlike his friends, I did not go overboard one way or the other. Something in me kept a bit apart and noticed the pattern. I did not do much more than provide a background affect field while noticing that both sides of the up and down might be part of one system, a see-saw unit over time. This might not seem like much, but it brought together climb-and-slide as a single movement, rather than splitting them into opposing choices (the counsel of friends was to pick one and reject the other, a "you can do it" frame).

I suspect this bit of "transcendental" vision had an impact in our being together, although I would be hard put to say how. In my imagination, I could see a baby tossed to and fro from heights of joy one moment to depths of agony the next, each state lasting forever. In the depths of my imaginings, there was a still point of awareness, a witness or seer who goes on seeing in the midst of emotional storms, even in the depths of madness.

Abe knew a good deal about his trauma history from AA, so interpretations I might make seemed redundant, although he appreciated my sense of his pain and faith in his potential. Perhaps he also appreciated my fear. I did not do anything special except try to be with him and say what I could.

The turn came little by little. He began to withdraw more and more from his life, from his girlfriend, work, AA. It took some time for me to notice he also was withdrawing from alcohol. It was a long and scary "dry" period. He became silent in sessions, although for a time he gave me some compass bearings, telling me that he was holed up in his room and did not feel like going out or doing anything. After a time, ever deepening silence, no compass, free fall. It felt less like a fall than being drawn down, sucked into the earth by an unidentifiable x.

I was scared not just for him but me. A young therapist, what would colleagues think if my patient killed himself? Would I get sued by relatives? Would I be brought up on malpractice charges? How could I let him fall this far? Shouldn't he get medical help? What was I doing? Was my practice on the verge of going through a version of Abe's pattern: just as it was getting started, it would end and I would wake up on the street, having to start from scratch or worse? Together, our lives would be ruined or ended.

After about eight months of going down the tubes and waiting, an amazing thing happened, something I was not trained for, an experience outside the domain of psychoanalytic therapy at that time. Abe began to report a radiant, compressed I-point. If it had a location, maybe somewhere in his chest. An ineffable, mysterious, pulsating point that he identified as his I. An indestructible I-kernel that went on I-ing. There was a certain amount of fear because of strangeness and unfamiliarity, but the overall feeling was reassurance, care, comfort, peace, permeated by radiant thrills, a core of pulsating aliveness in the centre of being. In months ahead, the experience expanded to include the outside world. Nature, people— aglow, pulsating, a caring centre everywhere. It was as if finding the safety of an indestructible I-kernel made generosity possible.

In time, I would learn more about spiritual experience and develop a broader mystical frame for psychoanalysis. I would not exactly call what I do mystical psychoanalysis, but it is not psycho-analysis deprived of mystical/spiritual sensitivity. Patients like Abe helped open me up, but it is also true that something in me needed this opening and was asking for it without my awareness. As this happened with Abe, I was out of my depth, or perhaps brought into it.

From my current perspective, I can probably pick out a few threads worth noting, but it is important to stress how at sea I was. One thread was my presence as a background subject. I was minimally intrusive, and although afraid, basically supportive. This is not an experience Abe had much of.

There was a lot of noise in Abe's life. He was picked on and abused by parents, although his mother provided moments of warmth. Her ups-and-downs paralleled his own later in life: warmth one moment, hell the next. His father was a heavy drinker who could piss on the living room floor in a stupor and not be aware of his cruelty. Neither daytime nor night brought Abe peace. Either was subject to violence in sudden shifts. The atmosphere he took in and adjusted to was one that included major doses of abusive care, cruel warmth. Abe's spirit remained trapped in his house, long after he abandoned it to save himself as a young man. You may guess that he, too, had an explosive temper that could turn on a penny, a hot rather than cold temper. He was not without heart. But that did not make living with himself or others easier.

I was a quieter person than he was used to, a quiet caring person. For him, it was like coming in out of the storm on the one hand, and an intimation that anything could happen on the other. If I was in unfamiliar territory, so was he. We had to find ways of being together. The unknown and unfamiliar was part of the basis of our relationship.

My being there for Abe in the background allowed something to pass between us. While I kept open as best I could while we were together, the impacts we had on one another were largely unconscious. While he and I were in the room and conscious of ourselves as separate people, I felt that most of our contact was unconscious. Part of this unconscious contact involved formation of a therapy bond, a bond made up of both of us which had an impact on both of us. A kind of mutual permeability worked within, behind, and under us, outside the margins of awareness. Perhaps within the margins as well, for, over time, we sensed something happening, although we could not say what. It became manifest, for one thing, in the surprise of his near-total withdrawal and surfacing of a radiant-I.

Related to the first thread was a second component. One thing inherent permeability can do is absorb good feeling over time. Surely, my attitude of quiet waiting had something to do with it. I was not entirely a negative background/foreground presence. I tried not to piss on his floor too often. And if I fell into stupor, I hoped it was not too oppressive. Bad as I was, I was generally a milder traumatic presence than his parents. Invisible good feeling in the background of our beings did me good as well. In a profound sense, we were supportive presences for each other, whatever else was in the mix (for a parallel later in my practice, see a list of therapy ingredients in *Toxic Nourishment*, 1999, Chapter Three, "Miscarriages", pp. 46–55).

Winnicott (1988, e.g., pp. 73, 76, 127–128) depicts variations in the emotional surround, variable, vibratory effects of changing emotional weather. Moment to moment shifts in the surrounding emotional weather for the infant make waves that spread through the infant's being. The way life feels shifts spontaneously, automatically, like instant to instant shifts in barometric pressure. So-called outside and inside worlds permeate and resist each other, forming part of unconscious life that supports and overturns. Buffeted by intermittent waves, we may not know why or how things happen or what they are. We do our best to ride them out, often going under, disappearing for a time that may seem eternal. The emotional seas that move through our being, supporting and dashing it, blend into a vast unit that forms the background of our lives (Eigen, 1986, Chapter Four, p. 154).

In Abe's case, inherent permeability and unconscious background emotional support were wounded. He was wounded as personality began to form: beginnings met with damage (Eigen & Govrin, 2007, pp. 44–58; Winnicott, 1992, p. 122). A pattern of damaged beginnings characterized important aspects of his life. When something good started, disaster followed, a devastating pattern beginning in infancy/childhood continuing into adulthood. The rhythm of no-drinking and binging followed this pattern.

Therapy supported a situation—blindly, mutely—in which Abe's psyche, in conjunction with mine, created a sequence wherein beginnings were sustained and led to something creative (sustaining is itself creative). One of the most creative moments of all was apperception of a radiant I-point that lifts existence. This experience occurred unexpectedly in a situation of extreme abstinence and contraction. Although it happened spontaneously, it seems likely that an excruciating birth process of many months paved the way; a process in which neither Abe nor I knew what we were doing or where we were going. We did not know we were participating in a creative happening. We did not know what kind of baby would be born or even that birth was in process. We went with it, no choice, whatever "it" was. It was hair-raising and I was filled with self-doubt, and if I had inklings that we were involved in something as significant as a personal revolution, I did not connect with them in any reassuring way.

I would like to try another partial formulation, based on Winnicott's writings on primary aloneness (1988, pp. 126–134; Eigen, 2007b, 2008) Winnicott posits an essential aloneness made possible by decent enough environmental support. This paradoxical notion states that a good sense of aloneness requires environmental support that the infant is unaware of. The very quality and being of the infant's sense of aloneness depends on the quality of support it does not know it is receiving. Without this support, inherent aloneness is wounded.

In many cases of addiction, individuals seek a reparative aloneness. For example, alcohol or drugs can substitute for environmental support felt as lacking. One seeks an aloneness supported by chemical changes in the hope of achieving a wholeness state the environment failed to enable. Too often, as in Abe's case, the results mimic environmental failure with repeated tastes of catastrophe.

I call the background support of primary aloneness *boundless, unknown support*. It seems to me that something like a sense of a boundless unknown is part of the background sense of existence. It provides a basis for emergent trust and faith. If one cannot trust the environment to uphold our beings, we live in jeopardy. And, indeed, a sense of jeopardy pervades our lives: both trust or faith and jeopardy, since all existence is thoroughly mixed. Bion's F in O is faith in the midst of catastrophe. We are linked together by faith and also linked (cemented in a fragmentary way) by catastrophe.

The environmental support our aloneness gets is necessary and remains part of our sense of aloneness all through life. We may not cognize it clearly, but it lives inside us, part of an indistinguishable nexus of support that feeds a sense of existing.

It is not unusual for primary support to be injured, even maimed. Addiction is one price we pay for wounded aloneness.[2] I do not think it is too great a liberty with words to extend addiction beyond alcohol and drugs to food, sex, money, power, and . . . (you fill in the blank). In a sense, war is an addiction that seeks to mimic, replay, and bring to awareness how catastrophic it felt as an infant when the world fell from under us, when the self fell apart or died for a time, perhaps a very long time. War apes a transient and macabre wholeness state, melding catastrophe with ideal hopes, wholeness incessantly blown up. Does it take war for some to acknowledge that faith can be wounded or is it that war mimics a wounded faith that happened long ago?

Therapy gave Abe's psyche a chance to let faith surface, regenerate, reshape. Not wholly perhaps, but more and a little better than before. In life, a little goes a long way.

There are many forms of mysticism (Eigen, 1998). Some emphasize union, some difference. Some emphasize self, some no-self. There is the saying that you have to lose yourself to find yourself and the co-saying that you have to have a self to lose it. Many aspects of the self–no-self journey can be highlighted. In Abe's case, personality contracted to a pulsating I-point, experienced as radiant and indestructible, an I-point going on being, emitting I-ness and is-ness. This contracted state was followed by an expansive, inclusive moment, starting with nature, then the radiance of all beings.

Some kind of "I am" experience has a long and rich history, creative and destructive. The Biblical God declares His name (or one of them) is "I am" or "I am I" or "I will be what I will be" or "I will be there," Krishna in the *Bhagavad Gita* reveals himself as everything everywhere, Self without limit. Abe's experience is humble by comparison, but real in its own right: an infinitesimal I-core leading to revelation of I-everywhere, all existence pulsating I. It was part of a process that initiated an essential change in Abe's life. He stopped drinking, got an apartment with his girlfriend (a huge move), made better use of AA and now, forty years later, is alive and well, living a decent life, a modest life, a good life, surviving himself in ways he can say yes to.

I would like to note some of the subtleties in Abe's mystical experience. A number of "elements" co-existed inside the experience: (1) a contracted I-kernel; (2) expanding I-radiance including all existence; (3) a sense of otherness in the radiant I and in the radiance of others, a sense of difference in meeting the radiant I-kernel and a sense of difference in the radiant otherness; (4) a sense of oneness or melding or union with both I and other; and (5) union or melding or indistinguishableness of both I and other. At the same time, the normal background of life continued, the world as we see it, cars, streets, buildings, things to do such as eating, sleeping, taking care of the apartment, answering or not answering phone calls, coming to therapy, and so on. All of this and more blended in Abe's experience. I tried to list some of the conjoined elements but it is very difficult to pin these things down. For example, does free-floating radiance precede the I, variably cathecting I and/or other? Does the I and/or other have its own inherent radiance? Is there both inherent radiance that precedes and makes possible perception of self and other and radiance inherent in self and other and in their emergence? It is important to emphasize the blend made up of so many mostly invisible threads. We see or imagine we see paradoxical tendencies in the mix, each nuance contributing to the colour of experience.

We have sketched distinction–union tendencies in both Abe's emergent experience and in the structure of the therapy situation. These tendencies take many forms, mostly silent, sometimes verbal. A background union, blend, bond in the therapy situation was partly rooted in contact with the unknown, an implicit contact hard to verbalize. This silent contact was part of the background that gave birth to experiences that changed Abe's life. We could not have predicted the experiences that emerged or their consequences. In a deep sense, Abe and I were birth attendants. Our co-presence was necessary for the birth to happen, although neither of us knew of the pregnancy until the baby was born. We can spend the rest of our lives learning about what we have given birth to in times of crises, a meaningful kind of learning. However, once the process is under way, births keep occurring and we can not keep up with them. We can only live them in piecemeal fashion, a little here, a little there, sometimes a little more. And every bit of this kind of living makes a difference to the quality of the whole.

Emergence of a sense of self and other, separately or co-arising, is one of the most creative experiences in life (for an early note on the generative sense of emergent self–other, see Eigen (1977)). So is the sense of the background they emerge from. There are ways one never loses a sense of the medium both self and other live in, although we would be hard put to say what it is. Perhaps we call it gestation, space, time, infinity, or all the processes an embryo or foetus goes through. Another ingredient might be all the life on earth that precedes and makes possible gestation. And all the processes that give birth to life. All these and more are part of the background bond of existence, the medium giving rise to and supporting you and me. The support itself is felt in the background, although we may or may not link up with it more consciously. It is sensed in the linings of our skin, nerves, and veins. Breathing brings us close to it. And with Abe, we do not know where it will take us, what it will do next.

A generative tendency permeates psychic foundations, inherent in nature. The Bible is filled with references to a new self, new life, a new day. One of Winnicott's most creative formulations has to do with emergence of a fresh sense of otherness (the "use of object" formulation, 1969; Eigen, 1981). Balint (1968) speaks of self–other mix-up, harmonious interpenetration which, if wounded, leaves a "basic fault" in a person.

My writing of union–distinction currents is one attempt to call attention to this double movement which, if we had equipment to perceive or think it, may be a single reality. Emergence of self–other is subject to mixtures of trauma and support. So is the "base" they emerge from. What happens to the background support of existence affects how life feels, the taste and scent and shape of self and other. We speak informally of being bent out of shape, in better or worse shape. If the trauma background has a severe enough impact, we can feel misshapen. The "we" itself contains union and distinction threads. We try to give voice to these threads as aspects of processes that generate us and that we play a role in partnering. As we voice them we live them, and they live us. They go on constituting us whether or not we speak them and this unconscious movement is part of the creative "feel" of living. The very birth of distinction–union tendencies is part of the creative sense of existence, dipping deeply into the unknown unborn. Is it too much to say of the latter that our sense of creativity would not be what it is without it? When I sense myself dipping into the infinitely unborn, I tingle all over. There are thrills no words convey, unless they are thrilling. Thrilling words touch the wordless thrill.

Distinction–union complexities

The word pathology has pathos and logos (spirit, study, science) built in. A study of suffering, linked with compassion, pity, path.

The question of what psychic pain is and how we respond to it is a major issue nowhere close to "solution". There are many stories about animals in pain, helpless to redress it. A helper comes to whom they are eternally grateful and a day comes when the helped one helps in return. These are charming portrayals of aspects of our predicament and the importance of helping each other, if only we knew how. Often our attempts at solution compound difficulties.

Our psyche is a source of pain as well as delight. We have psychic capacity for joy, horror, agony, fury—the whole gamut of emotional sensations. Psychic sensitivity is a source of suffering. Bion writes of the need to suffer experience. Staying with, living through, working with experience involves painful pressures. The capacity to support pressures necessary for digesting experience is itself in need of development.

I think of Michelangelo's sculptures, "Slaves" or "Prisoners" in Galleria dell'Accademia in Florence. We see figures emerging from the rock they are being carved out of. They are partly formed, partly semi-formed, partly emerging, partly embedded in the unformed stone, a birth or semi-birth in progress, permanently embryonic as well as in process of formation. They all are made from the same material that forms a permanent base and background, the inchoate unformed. A oneness of material gives rise to varied forms.

It is often said that these figures are good representations of Michelangelo's technique of sculpting forms by cutting away extraneous rock. I am not in a position to say that in this case, Michelangelo, in old age, attempted to give expression to the role the unformed plays in generativity, the unformed giving birth to forms and receiving them at the end. But I experience this and feel in these sculptures a sense of process that supports us as partly formed creatures that have little knowledge or control over who we are. Perhaps these works are confessional. The great Michelangelo, with supreme control over the rock he chisels, showing us his frailty, incompletion, mixed nature, partly individuated, deeply embedded.

A source of pain involves clinging to one or the other of dual states, exacerbating a conflict between embedded–emergent. On union–distinction planes, this translates to conflict between union–distinction tendencies. The situation is compounded when person-ality is subject to catastrophic impacts which affect these tendencies as well as other capacities. Pain that is felt is often mis-situated, a person misdiagnosing sources of psychic pain. In a traumatic impact, a complex system tears at itself and, partly, attempts to locate the pain "somewhere else" in the system. A system tears at its own complexity, attempting to break it down with the hope that it will rid itself of pain by breaking itself apart. Getting rid of pain or toning it down varies from displacement to vast nullifying of systems through which pain seems to arise.

One thing that can happen is that the dual tendencies split off from each other, or try to, as each side or tendency thinks the other is causing the disturbance and that by somehow tearing at or trying to wipe the other out or dissociate from the other the disturbance will be solved. Distinction imagines if it gets rid of union, disturbance will disappear, and vice versa. In response to difficulty, capacities may reach breaking points and repudiate or over-rely on each other. Co-dependent capacities may struggle not to be co-dependent, as if either tendency could have existence independently of the other.

Deformations arise in the struggle to persist. Each tendency "blames" the other for its difficulty, creating dramas of mutual attack and propitiation. Distinction, also, can blame itself and idealize union, and vice versa, leaving nowhere to hide, no safe haven except zeroing out—if that can be called safe. Systems and subsystems in turbulence sometimes seek zero hoping to reset or seek other paths.

In extreme form, the attempt to dislocate or blot out pain becomes a special case of a more general principle, that the psyche reacts to disturbance not just by striking out or hiding, but when these fail, resorts to trying to wipe itself out, as if getting rid of itself or part of itself will get rid of disturbance. This is a bit like God trying to rid Himself of disturbance by wiping out human existence in the hope of solving the problem of suffering. Get rid of psyche, no more psychic pain. In this vein, Freud felt flooding to be a primal trauma, whereas God thought it a solution. There is no contradiction. So far, life continues through the eyes of both needles.

In sum, distinction–union tendencies enter into many kinds of relationships with each other, antagonistic, symbiotic, parasitic, nullifying, disconnecting, nourishing. We can always ask what one or other of these tendencies is doing at any moment, since both are always co-present. They implicitly characterize mind–body as well as self–other relations and can be read on many planes, adaptive, psychic, behavioural, individual, sociological, mystical. To be permeable and distinct, connected and separate, in union yet distinct, is part of our plasticity and persistence, part of the mystery, difficulty, and creative challenge of our nature. Can we make room for ourselves? What quality of partnership with our beings can we work out? Each strand of our beings has a biography. Distinction has its history, as does union, as does their conjunction, their common fate. We mediate our makeup as it gives us ourselves. We are in process of learning if and how we and our makeup can evolve together in sustaining and nourishing ways. No invitation speaks to our creative core more.

Notes

1. The individual I call Abe here, I called Ben in the original publication (1973). Since then, I have used the name Ben for other people in other contexts and I thought it best to re-name him here, rather than confound him with other patients. The present chapter greatly expands on the original description.
2. In this clinical sketch I emphasized wounded aloneness. Wounded togetherness or union is also at stake but not focused on here. I picked a moment in our work when Abe reached for a deep alone point as a turning point. When trauma hits, damage is potentially widespread and it is unlikely that either term of distinction–union escapes it.

CHAPTER TWO

Spirituality and addiction

A connection between spirituality and addiction has been noted since ancient times. Closer to today, in the 1960s we heard a lot about drugs and transcendence. People took drugs and alcohol not only to escape, but to find themselves. Heroin, marijuana, cocaine, LSD, and alcohol opened the self, blew past the self, deepened the self, taking one to places one could not reach otherwise. Casualties were great, including psychotic episodes, hospitalizations, suicide, and compromised functioning. Yet, some gained from it, tasted great horizons, nourished creativity.

An issue was how to channel or control usage to optimize benefits and minimize harm. I have no idea how many solved this satisfactorily or how. Over forty years later, I have people in my practice with strong addictive tendencies and usage who function well enough, and even prosper, as creative beings. But I am also aware of wreckage, those destroyed by usage, and those who would have been destroyed without help. In this chapter, I am mostly concerned about this last group.

There is a story about Rabbi Akivah and the Kaballah, the latter likened to a garden, a kind of Eden. One man enters the garden and goes crazy, another kills himself. Rabbi Akivah enters and comes out refreshed, aglow.

There are people who need many years of support and work to touch something of this renewal. Some go through adumbrated versions of madness and death, living hells. Many fall through holes of self and taste ghastly agonies. Perhaps part of growth is to make room for suffering as a permanent part of living. At the same time, the beatific moment drugs seek is real, too. To become Rabbi Akivah is to live and assimilate something of the experience of the other two, those crippled by life's impacts, as necessary and valuable parts of the self.

One dare not say that all addiction is an attempt to taste spirit or qualifies as aborted spiritual experience or its proxy. But one cannot say that addiction may not have spiritual components and even, in time, give rise to spiritual struggle. Many addicts are looking to escape pain and fulfil yearning; some are trying to kill themselves, some are looking for moments of relief and uplift, for some it is part of a sense of degradation. Freud felt cigar smoking was part of his ability to be creative and it probably killed him (jaw cancer). Creative work, which many describe as addictive, often swings between grandiosity and disgust with what one does (or who one is) and substance abuse provides outlets and openings. Meditation, like creativity, is addictive and liberating and those who practise discover benefits and pitfalls.

Pain is part of life. Buddha began his great journey by facing the fact of suffering and penetrating some of its sources in the self. This journey continues today. Until this moment, the human race is challenged by the fact of suffering and not knowing what to do with it. Psychoanalysis lists many ways people avoid pain, including dumping it on others, adding to the sum of suffering in life.

Winnicott fingers a particular source of pain that strikes me as especially significant for addiction, at least certain aspects and forms of addiction. He writes of a basic aloneness that needs support for its full existence and unfolding (1988, pp. 131–134; Eigen, 2009, Chapters One and Two). Winnicott touches a moment when the infant in unaware that it is supported in life by the mother. Even a sense of being alone requires support one does not know is there. This situation, I feel, leaves a background sense of unknown boundless support throughout life. If something goes wrong with the support one does not know is there, the growing personality is affected.

Traumatized aloneness is a particular aspect of a more general formulation Winnicott (1992) made towards the end of his life, when he wrote of personality being hit by trauma as it begins to form. In my amplification, to be hit by trauma as one begins to form can turn beginnings into signals of trauma. One fears to begin (development, creative work, love) lest disaster comes. To begin is to court disaster, perhaps to seek it, at least to dread its felt approach. One may try not to begin or find oneself stalled as a way of avoiding catastrophe. If one dares to begin, one must deal with the dread of trauma hitting, which involves not just dread of death, but terrors of psychic deformation, deterioration, mutilation, pulverization.

Trauma may hit when one goes towards the other or when one is alone, unaware of the other's background support. The capacity to be with others or to be alone may be wounded. In the former, one may withdraw to nurse oneself, hide, regroup, or develop a paranoid underpinning, expecting injury when reaching out. A pattern of defensive isolation can develop. This is a different aloneness from the full aloneness (all-one) which has an implicit sense of unknown boundless support. If this support is in jeopardy, the possibility of contact with oneself is at risk, pressured, injured. Reactive fear, rage, isolation, or addiction to others can help one get through but thwart fuller unfolding.

Some quotes from Winnicott may help to get a sense of the background support for aloneness he brings to attention.

At the start is an essential aloneness. At the same time this aloneness can only take place under maximum conditions of dependence. Here at the beginning the continuity of being of the new individual is without any awareness of the environment and of the love in the environment which is the name we give (at this stage) to active adaptation of such a kind and degree that continuity of being is not disturbed by reaction to impingement. [1988, p. 132]

Throughout the life of an individual there continues a fundamental unalterable and inherent aloneness, along with which goes unawareness of the conditions that are essential to the state of aloneness. [ibid.]

From the point of view of the individual and of individual experience (which constitutes psychology) the emergence has not been
from an inorganic state but from aloneness; this state arising before
dependence can be recognized, dependence being an absolute
dependability. [*ibid.*, p. 133]

In my reframing, Winnicott heightens awareness of aloneness
supported by an unknown boundless other, the boundless
unknown, the unknown infinite. If experience of the latter is
wounded, aloneness is wounded.

* * *

Winnicott depicts an ideal state of perfect adaptation to an infant
who does not, cannot, acknowledge such support, a perfect
moment that remains as a memory of perfection, an ongoing sense
of the perfect. If support for this state is poor, defective, or
damaged, a state the infant needs to achieve suffers injury, in some
cases irreparably. Addiction repeats a sense of damaged perfection,
damaged beatitude. It tries to achieve a perfect moment that has
been marred and tries to heal the wound. The "healing" is only
temporary, more an attempt to make the wound go away, vanish for
a time, consign it to oblivion. Very like God tries to blot out the pain
(evil, disturbance) of the world by flooding it.

I must add as a qualifying note that Winnicott (and my use of
him) aims at a particular experience, one of a number of formative
states, and does not exclude mutual struggle, mutual adaptation,
and adjustments mother and infant make in order to succeed with
one another. My focus is on particular threads of experience and
threads of addiction. Injury to the special situation Winnicott conveys can play a role in lifelong recreation of a sense of unachieved
or damaged beatitude, a painless state one hopes will last forever.
Addiction makes an end run around the sense of damage but ends
up replicating and often adding to it. Pain and beatific threads
intermingle, meld, and become indistinguishable.

Addiction, in part, is a response to wounded aloneness and
attempts to find an aloneness without wounds, a wholeness of
aloneness not subject to damage. It seeks a state in which damage
did not happen, a taste of what it might have been like had a whole

alone feeling received the support needed for its existence. Since a drug, object, or behaviour pattern substitutes for this support, the experience needed for repair is missed. A substance or compulsion takes the place of going through the steps of addressing the wound aloneness bears.

Case 1. A case I wrote about before (1973, 1993; this book, Chapter One), here called Abe, brought home the importance of background presence in support of aloneness. I am aware that an adult case far removed from Winnicott's thoughts on infant experience must be taken metaphorically. Yet, metaphor conveys realities and, whether or not my speculations are "literally" true, they aim to mediate significant experience.

Abe was alcoholic, severe and chronic for many years. When I met him he was in Alcoholics Anonymous but still liable to find himself lying in the street after days of binging. Through AA he met a woman, but wounded the relationship with drunken fits and erratic behaviour. Nevertheless, the relationship endured. Without AA, I do not see how therapy could have succeeded. Yet, AA was not enough. The combined background of diverse sources of care changed his life.

The unfolding of his therapy was nothing I could have predicted. In AA and with me, he went over his trauma history: a rageful, frustrated, alcoholic father, an erratic mother, and a life of emotional storms. A damaged, damaging family atmosphere, not without warmth or love, but very wounded warmth and love that, at any moment, could turn into hell. Abe's alcoholism did not simply repeat aspects of his parenting, it also portrayed the wound at its centre. Quiet times were at a premium, often merely a cessation of storms or a kind of hiding. Genuinely alive quiet was rare and dared not come to fruition for fear of something breaking it.

There is an experiential arc or rhythm to genuine quiet. It evolves to a point where it completes itself and naturally ebbs, allowing the next wave of experience to unfold. It is rich, nourishing, peaceful quiet, akin to quiet immersion or gazing. I remember one of my sons as an infant gazing openly at nothing in particular, an infinite horizon, floating on an invisible background of peace. It is important that such moments do not suffer disruption. If allowed to play themselves out, a rhythm of experience grows. Background trust in implicit unfolding develops as moments of not getting derailed build and subside. For this to happen reliably, surrounding others must co-operate by not breaking the peaceful time unnecessarily. Sensitive co-operation and adaptation to mood tends to happen spontaneously and seamlessly, with no way for the infant to know that its time of peace and quiet depends not only on itself but on the ability of a caring milieu to tolerate and sustain it.

There was not much of a chance for this kind of quietness to develop in Abe's being. Therapy, by its nature, provided a more sustained taste of it. There is a background of caring, sensitive silence in therapy, in which the therapist tries to get a sense of the patient, a feel for who is in the room and what is happening, the mood of moment. A kind of supportive letting be, making room for the subjectivity of the other person. It is not an experience Abe may have had much of in his life, especially in his family.

I was not at first acutely conscious of the contrast between the therapy atmosphere and what Abe was used to, although I knew therapy brought many people into contact with new domains of experience. It took some time before the idea formed that, in part, binging to oblivion was a way of creating peace and quiet. The phrase, to get bombed, a term for getting drunk, combines wound and oblivion. To bomb oneself into oblivion adumbrates damage and a missing peace, a way to get a piece of "peace". Far from the open moment of the infant's gaze to the infinite horizon, but as good a substitute as Abe found on his own, given the pain he shut out. He bombed himself into helpless oblivion before he reached a point, asleep on the street, of resourceless dependence, at the mercy of the environment.

One finds ways of finding quiet moments, even if one has to destroy one's life to do so. Fortunately, Abe did not have to go this far, but he went far enough. As therapy unfolded, he withdrew from his various activities. He stayed home, rarely went out, stopped work, rarely saw his girlfriend, went to few AA meetings, then stopped altogether for a time. His isolation was alarming. Only later did it dawn on me that he was going to extremes to create the quietude he never had.

He kept most of his therapy appointments. We said little, but I asked about him, and we spoke a bit. He told me he was doing what he had to do, he did not know why. For a time, I feared therapy was having a dangerous effect. My dreaded fantasy—not impossible—was that he was caught in a gradient that might end in suicide. Was the contrast between therapy and what he was used to too much to bear? Only years later did I realize that I was a supportive background presence allowing aloneness to flourish.

The withdrawal lasted about nine months, gestation time. Abe came in and shared a visionary experience. His I contracted to an infinitesimal, radiant point that felt indestructible, as if something rock bottom was reached. In a short time, the radiance expanded or, more accurately, the radiant "point" was seen everywhere, coming from others, everything. All was bathed in radiance. One way I understood this was that when he reached a point of infinite value in himself, he experienced an inherent generosity that could see it in everyone.

At the time, I did not quite appreciate that I was in the mix. Without a supportive background presence that let be, that made room for him, he would not have had permission to experience this radical shift of centres of gravity. I suspect it was not just a matter of finding what was there and missed or damaged, but of enabling something new to emerge, something neither he nor I anticipated.

I realized that I did not know very much about varieties of spiritual experience and how the psychological and spiritual fuse. I experienced radiance, but not the way Abe described. Abe's hair-raising and successful sequence opened doors for me and was an invitation to grow in ways I could not yet imagine. It opened vistas for what therapy *could* be and *had* to be for some. A sense of unknown boundless support for aloneness, which Winnicott finds at times in the infant, is an important ingredient in the psychic mix that characterizes adult experience. Sensitivity to quietude is an inherent part of psychoanalytic background. The informing quality of background affective attitude affects the quality of quietude, the quality of aloneness. In Abe's case, it was a turning point. Binging stopped. He was "dry" all through the period of his withdrawal and return. His drinking days were over. I write this over forty years later. He has led a good life, a hard, real, and caring one.

*   *   *

Case 2. A woman, Wanda, with strong addictive tendencies entered therapy because she feared killing her daughter. Urges to kill her infant daughter mounted whether she was high or not, but she became most fearful that being high would release the possibility of actually doing it. When Wanda was high, she felt less in control. She more readily traversed the line from sensitivity to irritability to rage, especially when her daughter relentlessly cried and she was alone with her all day. She pictured throwing her baby against a wall, out the window, or stabbing her with a knife. Wanda most feared stabbing her baby to death. She several times found herself with a knife in hand, hovering over the crib. When she was high she felt boundless wellbeing and became rageful when it was aborted by her daughter's needs. She had no idea that having a baby would be so frustrating and bring her so close to the edge. She thought motherhood would be wonderful, like being high. She was not prepared for a baby to enter her life like a bomb.

Wanda deeply loved her daughter and the thought of what she might do horrified her. We worked on her family history, the pains– pleasures of her upbringing, the lasting wounds. Talking about her life in therapy took some pressure off. She did not realize she could talk about vulnerable areas without getting put down. By the end of the first year, the urge to kill her daughter diminished, and before the second year, the crisis was over. She grew into the pains of motherhood, the discomforts, fallibility, demands, and fatigue. She made room for real life and the fact that things are not the way one pictured. Having a special space for herself and her own inner being gave her more room.

One week she was suddenly seized by an acute realization of what she could have done, how close she came. It was something she often thought of, this time with special intensity. She wept and wept and when she looked up her face was glowing. She knew she might always be afraid of herself, yet a new happiness appeared. Life was moving on and she with it.

The night after this session Wanda dreamt that my face was aglow. It was not just my ordinary face but a radiant dream face that did not exist in waking life. Something like it exists in my feeling self. I feel, at times, profound radiance within, but what shows does not come close to inner reality. My radiant dream face uplifted her, ineffably so, and at one point she said, "It was as if my heart never beat before. It had been frozen in one place. Now it thawed and began to move." I thought of the prophet saying, "Turn your hearts of stone into hearts of flesh."

In session, it was *I* who had seen *her* glow. Her dream reversed and enlarged my experience. There are various ways to look at this. One is that we tapped into and shared a glowing place which manifested in different ways, as her, as me, but is more than both of us. As Abe discovered, it can manifest through all existence.

Unlike Abe's experience, the glow manifested first in the face of the other, rather than as I-kernel within. Abe, however, was not a father when I saw him. He did not fear murdering someone most dear. He was slowly killing himself. His, not a baby's, was the life he needed to save. He came to therapy because he feared for himself, rightly. Wanda feared for her baby.

Her baby could be viewed as an extension of herself and that would not be false. Yet, her baby reverberated deep inside her, in some sense was the deepest part of herself. It is an aspect of aggression that, in the depths, distinctions between self and other collapse. At the same time, her baby called her out of herself. She had to go beyond herself to tend to the needs of another who was not one with her insides. She had to stretch to encompass more than she bargained for. It is a paradox of parenthood that the baby is so inside and outside and requires new forms of personal struggle if one is to grow with the child.

Wanda greeted her baby with an array of drugs she took for years. She long enjoyed and suffered altered states and blackouts, relieving and alarming. Drugs relieved the great pain and stress she felt for much of her life, raised to new levels by parenthood. Wanda felt since childhood that something was wrong with her. Something inside was not right. There was no way to talk about it; she did not know what it was or what language was usable. Even if she could talk about it, she was sure bringing it up would make it worse. No one would know what she meant and she did not know either.

The urge to kill her baby propelled past lesser fears, forcing her to seek help that she feared would be useless, dumbfounded to learn that the thing with no name inside was not cast out. I did not know what it was either, but knew such states were real. For the first time, Wanda experienced shared awareness of it, whatever it was.

The glow I saw on her face after weeping was, I thought, profound relief that she and her baby survived each other. Perhaps melded with appreciation of the chances life gives and that help is possible. Therapy does not solve all problems and perhaps does not solve problems at all, but it gives a person support in face of herself. Her glow, I now feel, included appreciation of the fact that she and I survived each other, too, tinged with real gratitude. Her dream of me aglow touches a sense that good things *can* happen, a thawing moment of faith (variations of the experience of a radiant, glowing face are collected in *The Electrified Tightrope*, 1993).

In my inner vision, I saw the glow we shared touch wounds that never heal. She and I were wounded beings, deeply so, and such damage does not vanish. But being touched by the glow makes a difference. The damage takes less space, or, better, there is more space for other possibilities, with due respect for damage and damaging processes. At the same time, there is some healing, at times more than one believed possible.

Wanda's drug usage nearly stopped. She made moderate use of medication prescribed by a psychiatrist and for periods did without it. There was occasional drug usage, but much reduced. She lived a good deal of life by her own feelings, something not thinkable before. The mixture of struggle and glow, hard work and a sense of goodness opened paths and she took them.

At times, I feel there is a radiant face at the heart's centre. No doubt there are moments that the infant sees the mother as ineffably beautiful. There are beatific moments in infancy. The fact that this is possible testifies to a capacity that is ready to work all through life, if given half a chance.

*   *   *

Case 3. Sandra was in therapy much of her adult life. She had many therapists before me, but remained prey to serious binging–cleansing cycles, partly regulated by medication. In addition, she took painkillers to blunt psychic pain that tore through her life. She was addicted to painkillers, which she administered as she saw fit, making her cloudy and dull when she had to function in a clear way. She was aware that her semi-comatose states connected with how her mother often seemed to her. Through therapy, she saw that massive pain ran through her family and that each of its members developed ways of bypassing, coping with, surviving it.

We had come a long way and reached levels of trust–mistrust we could not get close to earlier. We survived a lot of mistakes and came through many difficulties. Then, one day, I made an error of judgement precipitating a crisis that unexpectedly led Sandra to a radically new experience of herself and life.

She urged me to say what I was thinking after she spoke about things that bothered her. My mind wandered to the trip I was going to take to South Korea, a real adventure for me. I do not know what made me think I could or should tell her, but I did. I was swayed by a sense of intimacy, an ease I imagined we felt together at the moment, a presumptuous ease. I told her I was thinking of the trip I would soon take and her fuses blew. She could not believe it. She was furious and hurt. How could I not be thinking of her and what she was telling me? She was sharing something important and I was thinking of myself? When she asked what I was thinking she expected me to comment on her life and what she told me. She could not believe I would be daydreaming about my trip. She could not get over it.

The session ended with her telling me I had better have something good to say for myself next time. She wanted me to think about why I did this, the reason for my inattentiveness, why I was not thinking about her. She wanted reasons for my behaviour. My assignment was to work on myself and give her an acceptable interpretation.

I thought about it during the week and had nothing to say for myself. In retrospect, I could see that feeling I could tell her what I was thinking should have been a signal not to, to be more mindful, at least to wait and see what grew. I acted precipitously, indulgently, mindlessly.

The next session began with her asking what I understood, what I came up with. I had not come up with anything satisfactory, but was feeling something more, deeper, unsure of what it was. In retrospect, it was, partly, a deeper feeling for Sandra, a sense of her life, her sensitivity, her journey.

She spoke of something off with us, something off between her and me. Then she added, "This something off, it's in all the parts of my life, my marriage, work, friends. I've always felt something off, something wrong from the start." After letting this sink in, she confessed that she wanted me to fix it, the off thing, fix *her*, just as she wanted to fix her husband, people she worked with, friends, family, mother, sisters and brothers, father. She wanted it all to be fixed, life to be fixed. Sandra concluded, "There is something broken in life and I want you to fix it."

I looked at her and deeply felt and said, "I'm broken."

Sandra responded, "I want to fix you."

"I can't be fixed," I said from my heart. "Whether you stay or go, I can't be fixed. Your staying or leaving can't fix me. I'm broken no matter what you do."

Sandra wept.

As she wept I added, "Always trying to fix things, fix the brokenness, the brokenness that is part of life. Yet in the centre of my broken heart is a golden radiant point, golden radiance."

At the next session, she came in feeling better and told of a profound experience she had on her way home from our last meeting. Two sayings moved her deeply. Sandra said, "It hit me as I left your office and started walking: *the way out is the way through.* I think that's Dante. The words filled me. They took me by surprise and seemed to say what we are doing. Then as I walked by the temple around the corner I saw a saying carved in stone above the door: *What does God want of you, but to do justice, love mercy and walk humbly with thy God.* I must have walked by that temple a hundred times and never noticed these words, never took them in. Suddenly they meant everything to me. I felt changed by them. They touched the way I really feel inside, the way I deeply feel but did not know I felt. I never knew words for it or knew such words existed. They are the most beautiful thing I ever heard. I stared at them a long time, wrote them down, walked home weeping."

These words from Micah are among my favourites, too. I have long felt them carved in my heart. The confluence between Sandra's opening and the way I felt when I first read these words opened a new domain of sharing. What a deep relief she and I felt. We had, indeed, come through something and both were grateful.

I saw Sandra in a new light. She had never shown herself as the kind of person who could be moved in this way. It was not just that I was being let in on another part of herself. She was, too. Micah, unexpectedly, opened a door she did not know she had, a point of contact with something deep and true and holy. Instantly, a sense of the holy suffused the pain of existence. In time, her use of painkillers diminished and ended. She tasted a new plane of possibility. She was horrified by what she had done to herself for so many years, all the feeling she killed off, life aborted. "I had to abort life to live life," she once said. Now she began to be her own midwife.

* * *

The three cases above express links between spiritual and psychological experience in different ways. In a way, spirit and psyche are indistinguishable. Yet, a distinction is made and I suggest holding it loosely. For many years, Buddhists consulting me expected to learn about their family history or, as Jung put it, individual or personal psychology. They somehow felt their spiritual practice was separate from psychological learning, the latter more a head thing, cognitive, a learning about. Their spiritual practice was the real thing. I felt this distinction odd, misplaced, and wondered at its origin. An overall goal is to diminish the split between spiritual and personal living, a task which always has been challenging, perhaps more so in today's driven and fragmented society.

In *Coming Through the Whirlwind* (1992), I presented two cases. A woman deeply into spiritual practice but at sea with psychological difficulties and a man who was a psychologist in need of spiritual experience. I hoped to convey how artificial this division can be. Working on one's psychology is spiritual and spiritual opening has deep psychic import.

I am tempted to use the term "incarnation" for the work I share here. Not just the spirit made flesh, but, in a way, the flesh as spirit. Inspirited flesh. We simply worked and what unfolded was a seamless mix of spirit and psyche.

The experiences emerging were part of processes partly accessible and partly unknown. For many centuries, a dominant thought was that higher processes imposed order on lower processes. For example, sensation was ordered by reason or judgement. Or, in Freud's case, tension between passion and reason required thought and work. Lower tends towards chaos or entropy, higher tends towards long-range vision, sublimation, and culture. It took time for an alternative idea, that processes spontaneously order themselves, to take hold. Freud incorporated the latter, too, but the old opposition between passion and reason never let go.

The view behind the work presented here hinges on spontaneous interaction of two beings, person to person, psyche to psyche, self to self. Emotional transmission spreads over time. The ordering is not from a higher place but from a psyche to psyche re-ordering, reshuffling, growing from interacting affective attitudes. We are permeable beings and affect each other. Over time, contact leads to changes. At the same time, critical moments that emerged for each person were their own creation, spontaneous happenings brought forth by their own being.

Each had moments of illumination, very personal, intimate, in which existence became new, fuller than before. Work first begins after such moments. Moments of opening make a difference but need to be mined. They may point one in better directions but the latter need cultivation.

Two of the people, Abe and Sandra, worked a lot on themselves before the turning points described. Struggle with their personalities resumed on a more meaningful basis. There is no easy way out of oneself. One must work with oneself all life long. But such moments as described here add to motivation, perseverance, patience, and care. In the cases above, moments of opening grew out of an interpersonal context. They might have happened without therapy, but in fact did not. Further work might have happened without therapy, but in fact therapy was needed to mediate the process, which continued in living after therapy ended.

All three individuals had wondrous experiences but it should be emphasized that peak moments, moments of opening, are partial. They may seem total at the time, but as their effects linger, more has to be done. They are like seeds that need farming, nurturing, work. In *Coming Through the Whirlwind*, I write of rebirth moments as a core structure of psychic experience. Not all rebirth moments bear fruit. Some are deranged and foster mayhem. Most are partly aborted. Even when we are born again we are partial births and partial abortions. We may keep trying to get it right, but frustration and constriction continues. A difference is that these latter become useful signals for further work and opening, perhaps even for profound compassion and acceptance. The despair they were part of becomes a smaller player as "coming through" rhythms deepen. Faith and opening take hold as a deeper part of life and provide a context for work that must be done.

CHAPTER THREE

I don't know

My purpose in writing this chapter is to dignify and celebrate the phrase, *I don't know*. It has a long, rich cultural heritage. Yet, in political practice and everyday life, it often is denigrated, as if those who seek or hold power, whether in family, work, or politics, are phobic about not knowing. They fear that appearing not to know would compromise their position and precipitate a slide down the ladder of esteem.

We are urged, from school on, not to be ashamed of not knowing. We are told that not knowing makes learning possible, part of the process of getting to know. Yet, few of us escape childhood without being shamed for not knowing. I doubt many go through school without many kinds of humiliation, not least involving damage to fear of not knowing.

We learn early to cover up deficits. An illiterate delinquent may hide his incapacity with increased bravado and destructive acts. It is a funny kind of learning, making believe we know more or are better, stronger or more able than we know we are. I remember volunteering to tie someone's shoelace in kindergarten, although I did not know how. The teacher treated me rather well, but the event stuck like glue in my mind. I wondered over many years why I had the need to do that. I knew I could not tie the shoe. Yet, I needed to seem as if I did, even though the result must be failure. I was caught between fantasy and reality, hung by my own mind.

When I see world leaders making destructive decisions in a show of power, I wonder what gaps, deficits, ignorance, and weakness they push away. Do they imagine they know more or are more capable than they are? Do they overestimate ability to gain a hoped for outcome? Sometimes it appears that fear of showing weakness and ignorance becomes more important than constructive action and going through processes the latter entails. Hallucinated strength and ability—hallucinated right and might—becomes more important than what reality can bear.

What a relief when someone says, "I don't know, wait. There's more to learn. Let's make an opening for learning." I don't remember a single public declaration of uncertainty and need for deliberation in high government decisions in the past eight years—momentous decisions affecting lives, bodies, souls (I write this in October, 2008, on the threshold of a crucial presidential election in the USA).

*   *   *

Not knowing does not sit well in high places, yet, all through history, kings have needed advisers. There is the famous story of Bodhidharma allegedly introducing Buddhism to China (Cleary & Cleary 2005, Case 1). In his crossing from India to China, Bodhidharma meets Emperor Wu, a good ruler with many merits and positive practices. Emperor Wu asks Bodhidharma, "What is the essence of the holy teachings?" "Emptiness without holiness," Bodhidharma replies.

Emperor Wu is taken aback, perplexed, uncertain, perhaps insulted or challenged, perhaps "assaulted", the twinge felt when internal ground shakes during personal exchange. To be empty, not holy? What about goodness, merits, virtues?

One can imagine the Emperor trying to keep his cool. Maybe he is reeling, maybe Dharma appetite is stimulated. "Who are you?" he asks. Bodhidharma answers, "I don't know." The emperor pauses, perhaps a bit shocked, afraid of losing face, a deer caught in headlights, unsettled, unsure, paralysed, needing time to regroup and sort things out. The moment passes and he fails to reach out for instruction. Bodhidharma goes his way.

Later Emperor Wu asks a teacher about the event. "Do you know who that man is?" asks the teacher. "I don't know," replies the Emperor. "He's the bearer of the Buddha heart–mind seal," the teacher says. Then adds, "Don't bother sending after him. The whole kingdom couldn't bring him back."

A moment gone forever, yet it leaves waves. Emperor Wu is not immune. He opens. Not in time for the missed encounter. But the encounter leaves residues, something begins. Two different "I don't knows", with different functions, levels, and possibilities. The Emperor's "I don't know" is both seed and barrier, a fence around himself. Yet, there are seeds of not knowing to cultivate. It is not impossible for the Emperor's "I don't know" to shed shells and become the radically open not-knowing Bodhidarma mediates.

* * *

Legend tells us that, after leaving the Emperor, Bodhidharma went to another part of China and sat meditating in front of a wall for nine years. I suspect the wall is a wall both Bodhidharma and Emperor Wu share, and that you and I share with them. A wall of self, a wall surrounding self, a wall that keeps us walled off. There are moments when the wall gives way and we taste wall-less existence. Such naked moments make us more ready to work with walls.

* * *

One of the great naked moments in cultural history is expressed in the Book of Job. Everything is stripped away, family, wealth, health, and honour. Job is pictured sitting on a dung heap cursing the day he was born. Everything he valued, everything he thought made life worth living—gone.

Friends spout scripture to rationalize his bad fortune and justify God's ways. Surely Job's misfortunes are payback for sins, God's medicine for improvement. No matter the deaths of wives and children and flocks. They are part of a karmic magical show challenging the depths of Job's being, a growth experience.

Job rejected his comforters. Ordinary wisdom did not ring true in face of his suffering. He could find no moral or reasonable justification for the horror of his existence. What could justify this agony?

God offers no justification. He simply shows Himself. He cows Job with the display of creation. Look at all God can do—sea beasts, the teeming earth, light and darkness, good and evil. More than cowed, Job is awed by the immensity of existence, the bare fact of being. God's show of power blows a hole through him. Talking with his Creator brings unsuspected moments of illumination, new levels of intensity, realization. Suffering and loss perforate experience and bring him to immediate God-contact. There is nothing left but God. Job and God. You and God.

There are many ways to read this story. We can be horrified at the casual sacrifice of life for the sake of one man's egocentric journey. We recoil at Job cowed by God shutting him up by a display of power, showing him who's Numero Uno—a myth imbued with struggle with authority, power, and helplessness.

My reading is more a mystical fairy tale. The loss of life expresses loss of parts of the self, investments of self, divestment of attachments until one reaches a point of ultimate aloneness, faces God alone. Near the end of Jewish religious services a song is sung that says of God, there is nothing else.

It is an important moment, to reach this place. To taste, dip in, live it, a depth reality. How to reach God? Plotinus says, "Cut away everything." In a Flannery O'Connor story, a fundamentalist Christian dies and goes to meet her maker, surprised that even her virtues are burned away. The mystery goes deeper than everything in us, deeper than everything we are.

A mystical fairy tale. Job's loss of family, wealth, possessions expresses a movement of contraction to a pure pain or null point, where only pain and nullity exist, an unbearable point through which God appears. After reaching the Divine, an expansive movement begins, represented by new family and flocks, fuller life returning, body filling out, psyche filling out. A null movement followed by opening. The psalmist says, "I go to sleep weeping and wake up laughing." So much more so with Job (Eigen, 1995, pp. 191–192).

These are momentous movements, shifts of attitudes, states. Bible stories adumbrate what Bion, after Hume, called "constant conjunctions": experiential tendencies that appear together, attempts to locate inner tendencies, aspects of our makeup, bits of who we are, what we do, how we work. We can read in Bible stories aspects of our makeup, tendencies, and counter-tendencies. In a way, silent films and Bible stories have something in common: portrayals of disturbance and disturbing events. When Laurel and Hardy begin a film saying, "What a beautiful day", you know that is a signal for disasters on the way.

The drama of Job brings him to a point of not knowing. Maybe he thought he knew something about life. He was a good man and good actions led to a good life. Then the ground of ordinary learning and morality was stripped away. What he knew or thought he knew availed nothing. He could not solve the problem of pain and disaster. His prior "solutions" dissolved. The domain of not-knowing opened new experiential planes. Life would not be the same after his rock-bottom shake-up and meeting God face to face. The story of Job encodes inner realities of urgent concern.

* * *

A usual translation of a key passage in Job is "Yea though He slay me, yet will I trust Him". It is at a point when Job is brought to realization. He sees through the mists of usual concepts of morality, expectations, and understanding. He has come through the null point and reached God. What the mind thinks and believes is nothing compared with this direct, immediate experience. Here is total trust and faith. In life? Mystery? God? An unknown, mysterious power that he now knows, in the sense that he has made contact with it, reality itself? A reality such that even knowing some sense of it is a radical unknowing, a radical opening. No matter how one knows or how much one knows, there is more. Even to be surfeited and filled is always a beginning. In another moment Job makes clear it is not "brain" knowing, not conceptual knowing or belief: "From my flesh, I see God" (19: 26). A seeing with his being, not with eyes alone.

In a contemporary, alternate translation of the trust passage, Mitchell (1992) writes something like: "Though you slay me, I will not stop arguing and fighting with you, I will not stop asking you to justify yourself, I will not let you off the hook by your display of shock and awe". God requires autonomy. The injured soul seeks an accounting to the bitter end and beyond. There is no reason to let go one's sense of justice, no need to capitulate to tyranny or other forms of force and bamboozlement.

My mother went to her death saying she had questions for God that God best answer, foremost among them the death of her child, my brother, when he was ten. She never stopped questioning God for this incomprehensible, maddening horror. Mitchell captures her state and the just claim of tortured humanity.

The story of Job takes the skin off our souls. What direction shall we take in our nakedness? Some go one way, some another. Each contributes. Put all our paths together and we get some picture of human potential, for better, for worse. As a minimum, we need capacity to respect differences in mourning, differences in faith.

*   *   *

Buddha notes that suffering is a fact of life. One must acknowledge it. One must feel it, know it. An odd kind of knowing, as frequently one suffers without knowing why. That Buddha calls us to experience our suffering suggests that we may not do so, not fully, not openly. Psychoanalysis teaches that suffering can go underground, be displaced, numbed, deadened, mislabelled. And that rerouting or playing down our suffering, whatever its advantages, brings its own kinds of pain. From Buddha's standpoint, many of us need to be brought into contact with our pain and suffer it as a moment of honesty, of faith, of possibility. At the very least, we need practice in building tolerance for our states, at least up to a certain point.

Buddha does not pretend to solve the great metaphysical mysteries of life. He avoids questions from students that try to pin down such a frame. Buddha sticks with experience, as best he can. There are, too, cultural biases, practical hierarchies, cosmological ethics and, as Buddhism developed, institutional codes. But what I would like to emphasize is a thrust towards experience. We suffer. Old age, loss, illness, death, poverty, psychic inflation, and a keynote of Buddhist psychology: attachment to our desires, to ourselves, a nodal point of pain.

A story is that Buddha discovered rampant suffering when he went outside the palace he grew up in, and committed himself to overcoming it. I picture him focusing on his own pain, an avatar of suffering humanity, as if empathically contacting the suffering of others brought him face to face with pain inherent in life itself. The focus on inner pain became more and more intense until the psyche burst and another field of experience opened: nirvana, beatific experience, void, emptiness, freedom. To be free of self, free of desire, free of loss and gain: the freedom of opening.

On an elemental plane, this movement is a raw arc of experience, a basic rhythm. A story with infinite variations and forms, on all levels of human existence. Buddha adds an ethical dimension to the path he points to. Not only meditation or concentration, but right thought, action, work. We continue as one life form or another until we manage to transcend ourselves and restructure our existence with a truly caring attitude. Many capacities and dimensions intertwine in constant interplay on the way.

What I want to emphasize here is the elemental movement: suffering ↔ nirvana. Job's suffering ↔ opening is a profound variation of this rhythm. Buddha's "solution" is a practical one. It takes place on the plane of experience and works with inherent movements between suffering and cessation of suffering. This basic pattern has roots in infancy, an experiential circle that occurs over and over, alternations of pain–distress and rest, movements between agony and peace, hell and heaven, unbearable tension and just going on being. But when one says, "roots in infancy", what can one mean? Why these roots, for this kind of being? Why this kind of being?

It may be that Buddha's discovery of an elemental experience became encoded in increasingly complex cognitions and practices, as is the case with elemental experiences in any cultural domain. Whatever the differences between Buddha and Job, they point to an experiential rhythm that can be focused on in its own right, teased out of theories that frame them. Neither solves questions of why life takes this form, why you and I are here and not other unborn possibilities, or how and why anyone came to be at all. Buddha and Job alert us to what our equipment can do, possibilities it offers. Job in his sitting, Buddha in his, bring us to points of opening. And when we touch this discovery, opening does not stop.

*   *   *

The "I don't know" of identity. What a freedom to not know who I am, and not have to know. Yet, there is widespread public dread of not knowing who one is. I have no idea what statistics there could be that would accurately number how many people partly fake identity. There is great pressure to pretend to be a person, some kind of person with a specific identity. In my own life, it took many years for the taboo against not knowing who I am to diminish. At certain junctures, it seemed sinful not to know. "You don't know who are you are?" Then comes a list of ways to know and things to do.

*   *   *

Shakespeare tells us, "to thine own self be true." He puts this wonderful line and those that follow in the mouth of Polonius, whom critics describe as fatuous, clownish, and banal. Polonius may not be the deepest and most commanding of personalities, but he tries to be a good father in his way, and in his own way cares. He is not a bad man, certainly not one of the evil doers, if not an exemplary figure. One wonders how to take his words, echoes of the ancient oracle: "Know thyself".

Polonius would not be one's first choice as a signifier of self-knowledge. It is impossible to picture him daring to upset the underpinnings of his personality in such a quest. One may be moved by what he says, but must take the saying with a grain of salt, the more chilling to realize that the son he advised was killed, as was he, and his daughter killed herself. So much for wise parenting.

But then Socrates, whose life was a meditation on the oracle's words, did not end well either. Still, his dying words, as portrayed by Plato, are alive today, his life an exemplary quest. "Know thyself," says the oracle and Socrates peels onions of beliefs, opinion, and thought. Sometimes, I say to a patient at the end of sessions, "Love thyself." A mix of Polonius, Socrates, oracle, and therapist? Can I be sure of what I mean, how deep, how real, how banal, how suspect, how cautionary? At times, love is direct, immediate, palpable reality. Sometimes, saying it creates it, calls it into being. Perhaps I or someone or something in me senses it, a dim, urgent background presence, and naming births it. At such moments, saying "Love thyself" is an act of faith, and faith a kind of birth.

We are encouraged to find our true self, our real self. There are moments when this feels possible, moments when it seems to really happen. We hit pay-dirt and the state resonates with further states to come. At other times, such moments are followed by criticism, questions, seeing constructions, beliefs, conditionings, experiencing doubts. Self-questioning is productive, yet not the only vehicle. With a sweep of a psychic eraser, whoosh, gone. Moments of radical openness.

At times we see a question mark in the heart of identity. When I was young, this question was an axe to chop phoniness away. I revelled in Socrates saying that he knew that he did not know, that he was ignorant. As I got older, not knowing who I am became a friend, welcome, freeing, serene. Blissful time of no-self or, at least, the possibility of taking myself less seriously. Such relief to be free of self, if only for moments. Moments spread.

*   *   *

Jesus associates not knowing who we are with forgiveness, "Forgive them, they don't know what they do". He is on the cross when he says this, facing death and perhaps a more devastating kind of aloneness, "Father, Father, why have you forsaken me?" Is there a connection between undergoing the depths of forsakenness, radical aloneness (all one, alone) and forgiveness? The agony of radical abandonment coupled with a surge of compassion. Buddha mediates a parallel stream, letting go all attachments, everything one holds on to and that holds one, attachments to life, to death, opening to a saving void transcending identity, liberation expressed in compassion for all beings.

Jesus says, "Forgive them." The grounds he gives is not knowing, or, in Buddha's terms, ignorance. There are differences between forgiveness and compassion worth investigating, but here I wish to emphasize their link. Forgiveness as part of compassion and compassion as part of forgiving (giving-for; for-giving). To give to others. In the case of Buddha and Jesus, to give to others what one finds most deeply oneself. Compassion and forgiveness linked to some form of ignorance.

They do not know what they are doing. This is the same thing God told Jonah when Jonah was miffed about the predicament God placed him in. He felt God made him play the fool. "If I go to the people and tell them to repent, they'll listen and you won't destroy the city and I'll look silly." But God made it nearly impossible for Jonah not to play the prophet and Jonah did as he was bid. "Woe, doom to your whole city, God will wipe it out and everyone in it, if you don't change your ways!"

Just as Jonah feared, the people listened and God repented of his wrath and Jonah was bitter. Jonah did not have the same profound acceptance of his destiny as Jesus. He sat on a hill outside the city hoping to see it destroyed, knowing it would not be. He argued with God and God reasoned with him. "You did your job. They heard you and became the better for it. Should I destroy these precious beings who don't know their heads from their assholes?" For the moment, God valued creation, human beings and all they built and all their crops and animals. And Jonah, sulking, had to meet the challenge of himself and struggle for self-transcendence. He did well in spite of himself, but there was more to go. He was placed in a predicament that rubbed his nose against his ego and he did not know what to do with himself. He did not solve his sulk but we suppose life went on and he with it, one way or another. Jonah glimpsed the more beyond himself. He was on talking terms with God and ran, evaded, argued, and passed the task of struggling with myopic, self-centred views to us.

Jesus' locution, too, leaves questions. *They* do not know. Jesus models compassion with a kind of distancing: they, over there, not me. This often is the form forgiveness takes. The other is the one who needs to be forgiven. But do I? Yes, I do, on multiple planes, by other people like myself, by God, by myself. Is my not knowing what I do adequate grounds for forgiveness? If so, the worst me, malignant me, may be getting off the hook.

One could turn this and say, if I can be forgiven just because of ignorance, wouldn't the evil in me warrant compassion even more so? All the hidden nooks and crannies need compassion and forgiveness to seep in, all the places I cannot find or go to.

One of the biggest challenges is to go from *they* to *I* or *we*. Forgive us, for *we* do not know what we are doing. We do not know who we are. The move from they to I/we involves profound inner reordering, new planes of freedom, quest, and caring. Not *they* do not know. *I* do not know, *we* do not know.

Notes on Bion's "I don't know"

Not knowing is an important part of psychoanalytic methodology. Freud, informally, wrote that he did not know where a sentence would end up when he began it. His writing twists and turns, marked with illuminations. In his letters to Fliess he writes that he is following his unconscious, letting the horse lead the rider in a process of discovery. Yet, over time, his insights gather around persistent nuclei that are codified in conceptual networks.

When I entered the psychoanalytic world, Freud's thought seemed set and formulaic. Only when I dipped in for myself did I begin to appreciate the tangle of interlocking and antagonistic whirls of vision, thought, and possibility that close reading unveiled. War between primal elements envisioned by ancients seared the work of Freud, together with a sense of deep symbiosis between warring capacities. At the same time, there were loose ends to pull, ambiguities to plunge into, worlds within worlds to explore. I did not know until it grabbed me from within how thrilling reading Freud can be.

His advocacy of free association and free-floating attention add further dynamism to the role of not knowing in psychoanalytic work. Freud is often criticized for seeming to know where free association and free-floating attention will end up, a more codified psychoanalysis displacing a more open one. But the difficulty, pain, and thrill of letting go usual "controls" and letting the mind go where it will is an addictive discipline that can lead to lifelong enrichment.

Bion amplifies Freud and goes further. He describes the psychoanalytic attitude as being without memory, expectation, desire, or understanding. A radical openness he calls faith. A special kind of faith he expresses as F in O, where O is unknown, ultimate reality, in this context, an emphasis on psychic reality, ineffable, infinite: "The fundamental reality is 'infinity', the unknown, the situation for which there is no language—not even that borrowed from the artist or the religious—which gets anywhere near to describing it" (1994, p. 372).

In the sentences preceding this passage, Bion speaks of a crisis of faith, a "crisis of 'I' and 'You', or 'We' and 'They'", a crisis that requires going beyond opposition and symbiosis, predator–prey, and usual attachment language to a love that terms like 'love of God', and 'absolute love' only hint at, a love of reality that requires a language for the infra- and ultra-sensuous. A language one can only hint at, between the lines.

Bion gives as an example the artist who paints a street in Delft that conveys a reality no one has ever literally "seen". One "sees something that is quite different from any brick wall or little house that he has ever known or seen in his life" (*ibid.*).

We slide into tricks of words and capacities. We have been speaking of not knowing, but seem to touch a knowing of reality that is direct experiencing, direct apprehension, immediate contact with "something". One gets the feel of it, a sense of it, but what is this sense, this feel? Once we slide into beliefs, arguments, oppositions we are somewhere else.

If we do not take our opinions and maps for the thing itself, talking about it, trying to communicate it with colour and words can be worthwhile. More than worthwhile. Grappling with it and expressing it creates more of it—more reality and vehicles of approach. At the same time, in face of our acquisitions, can we remain ready to go back to square zero and not use hard-won perceptions and apprehensions as weapons to close doors or, worse, bash ourselves and others?

Where does non-violence start? Is it possible? Where does one need to go to find it?

*   *   *

"I don't know" in psychoanalysis was often taken as a sign that the patient was defensive about something, perhaps resistant to further unfolding or contacting difficult material. Fliess (1971) associated it with rips in the person's psyche, unspeakable, unknowable trauma. One does not know because one does not want to know or cannot know. Psychoanalysts often treated not knowing as motivated. This does not mean that not knowing is always motivated. That would be a caricature. It does mean it *may* be motivated, that is, connected to trauma, conflict, and defensive needs.

I noted above that Bion connects not knowing to the psychoanalytic method, a radically open not knowing. Yet, he also sees that not knowing often has a motivated component. In one passage (1994, pp. 222–224), Bion felt that a patient saying "I don't know what I mean" used this state and locution self-protectively, fearing attack from the analyst modelled on figures in his past.

Bion goes more deeply, associating the patient's fear with fear of emotional experience generally. To an important extent, our emotional experience makes things feel real. The patient's "I don't know", in this instance, is an index of a freeze put on feeling: ". . . the patient fears that if he learnt anything from his emotions, he would learn that he is alive. . ." And with emotional aliveness comes a whole panoply of feelings that the patient may not yet be able to acknowledge, let alone bear, sustain, or digest.

Freud spoke of flooding as an early trauma (e.g., flooded by stimuli, sensation, feeling). He spoke of hating painful states and trying to eject them, get rid of them, or tone them down (e.g., hallucinate them away). Bion suggests his patient hates emotions (because of their potentially devastating consequences) and cannot digest them. If he cannot rid himself of them, he is stuck in chronic emotional indigestion. In effect, he tries to get rid of the aliveness of his life. In this case, the very aliveness of life makes life indigestible, intolerable, dreadful.

"I don't know" can cover up a set of processes in which potential aliveness is rendered blank. The press of feeling becomes an empty cipher. "I don't know" becomes a nothing suspended over dangers in one's dreams. Bion, too, associates this state with fear of insanity and, more, the discovery that, in important ways, one *is* insane.

"I don't know" can be a huge suitcase hiding a lot of sins or a guiding point for the openness of analytic work. It is not unusual that a psychic state is multi-faced.

* * *

Bion often speaks of double tendencies as parts of a process. In a talk he gave in New York City in 1978, he spoke of learning that a tank's metal can feel like jelly when you are inside and shells are falling, and that when you are afraid—and in war you always *are* afraid or should be—it is as easy to get killed running away from as running towards the enemy. Many years later he wrote something similar with regard to emotional truth, from which one runs away and towards, truth one fears to know yet feels one must know, truth about one's life. Levels of not knowing and profound, if obscure, knowing are compacted. A biblical observation that one hand does not know what the other is doing touches this. That we are multi-ocular and also blind is one of tantalizing paradoxes of our experience.

We cannot catch emotional transformations in the act. We can not *know* O, we *are* O. In one compressed attempt at communication, Bion writes (1970, p. 46):

> Although O (infinity) is inaccessible to K it is perfectly accessible to T in O. The analyst has to become infinite by the suspension of memory, desire, understanding. The emotional state of transformations in O is akin to dread as it is represented in the formulation:

> > Like one that on a lonesome road
> > Doth walk in fear and dread;
> > And having once turned round moves on,
> > And turns no more his head;
> > Because he knows a frightful fiend
> > Doth close behind him tread.

> The 'frightful fiend' represents indifferently the quest for truth or the active defenses against it, depending on the vertex.

In the situation Bion depicts, what is known, what is not? He reaches deep in the well, calling the naked attitude he expresses faith. It is as if a certain kind of faith peels the skin off the psyche and opens a world of raw impact and transformation, a substratum of emotional experience seeking and undergoing transformations. When we wake up into K we wonder—did we dream it, is it real?

*   *   *

Another of Bion's favorite quotations is Keats on negative capability:

> I had not a dispute but a disquisition with Dilke on various subjects; several things dove tailed in my mind, and all at once it struck me

what quality went to form a Man of Achievement, especially in Literature, and which Shakespeare possessed so enormously—I mean Negative Capability, that is, when a man is capable of being in uncertainties, mysteries, doubts, without any irritable reaching after facts and reason. [John Keats, Letter to George and Thomas Keats, 21 December 1817, quoted by Bion, 1970, p. 125]

Here is a very pregnant "I don't know", akin yet a foil to the nothingness in which the poet sinks in the poem, "When I have fears that I may cease to be". Dazed by the immensity of time and existence, and the fear that he "may cease to be / Before my pen has glean'd my teeming brain", the poet enters a meditative state in which "I stand alone, and think, / Till Love and Fame to nothingness do sink".

The letter's radical immersion in pregnant not knowing and the poem's dizzying contemplation of ultimate loss represent two kinds of emptiness: teeming existence and its unknown processes and fecundity linked with vanishing without a trace. Both threads nourish creativity.

*   *   *

Levinas (2000; Eigen, 2005), akin to Bion and Keats, emphasizes sitting with the unknown and unknowable. As he puts it in one passage,

... a new attitude ... the search for a proximity beyond the ideas exchanged, a proximity that lasts even after dialogue has become impossible. Beyond dialogue, a new maturity and earnestness, a new gravity and a new patience, and, if I may express it so, maturity and patience for insoluble problems ... I have the idea of a possibility in which the impossible may be sleeping. [pp. 87–89]

Levinas's is at once a language of contact with others and self and with insoluble crises, disturbances, difficulties. Proximity beyond differences, proximity in-differences. Sitting with the insoluble evokes unsuspected growth. One kind of growth involves a deeper sense of shared humanity, proximity beyond disagreements about what we know or think we know, beyond the will for possessions, territory, beyond beliefs mistaken for faith.

*   *   *

There are seemingly endless cultural resources related to aspects of not knowing. Cloud of unknowing, dark night of the senses, *amor dei*, godhead transcending concepts, circle with centre everywhere, perimeter nowhere, *Ayin Soph*, infinity, awesome sense of Mystery.

A Hebrew children's song: "Hashem is here, Hashem is there / Hashem is always everywhere / Up-down, all around / That's where he can be found".

There is no bottom to reach.

Dip and you will find.

*   *   *

We reach states in which we wonder, "How *can* we hurt each other?" Can we be sure that we are who we think we are? Can we be sure of our "rightness"? What do we know about the contraction and pulse we call ourselves?

To not know who we are or who God is—isn't that releasing? It makes room. What if God does not know either? That would be a freedom they do not teach in school, church, or public life. To imagine God omniscient or omnipotent is short-sighted. Such pinched ideas put God in a straitjacket.

More room in our own straitjacket will not end injury, but it is a start. Making room is a path, not a finality.

*   *   *

In the Bible, when asked his name, God says, "Tell them *I am* sent you." Or, perhaps, *I am what I am* or *I will be what I will be* or *I will be there*. I will be there for you. I am here for you.

I think God understood the difficulty of this communication. He tried rules, commandments, external guides, mystical visions. His prophets said find your heart, the heart within the shell of your heart, a heart of flesh and blood. A beating heart, a heart that feels. All the laws of goodness are imprinted there, in a point no bigger than a thumbnail, an infinitesimal point.

What is good?—no easy matter. No one solves the tangle of mixed realities. Yet, a template or thread exists in the expressive face, the feeling heart. Wait, listen, sense. Feel the intimacy.

When I was in my thirties and all alone, sometimes I would wake up in the middle of the night saying, "I love you." Who was

I speaking to? Where did these words come from? It is easy to guess and make up answers, but I do not know. They opened a deep place.

Today I often feel an "I love you" presence while awake. The deep place in the night is spreading.

* * *

Our formulas are tries. It is hard to get under them once they grab hold. Sometimes it helps to put a lot into zero and give yourself time. Put everything you can into zero, all your divisions, to the extent you can. Become zero with all your might. Give your all. Something happens.

Who or what one thought one was becomes less relevant than a hermit crab's shell. A living moment makes one say, "Thank you." To whom?

God's model, "I will be there—I am here" applies to us, too. Whoever I am. Whoever you are.

* * *

God/no-god. Self/no-self. Either way, openness to endless fecundity. What kind of I am I saying when I say I am here or when I say Openness is here? O for Open, a name of God/no-god in our time. Opening as a path.

What if the whole human race opens all at once, everywhere at all times for one moment?

* * *

How can one go through life in a state of not-knowing? When we greet each other and ask, "How are you?" and hear, "I don't know" life would grind to a halt. Better not let not-knowing infiltrate too far.

Yet, the cat is already out of the bag. "I don't know" is part our nature, part of our freedom, part of our caring. "I don't know" plays a role in structuring us, including our misuse of it and defences against it. We try to shut it down, keep it from spreading, from overturning all structures and hard-won knowledge.

It is a pole of our being, not the whole of it. Placed rightly, it sustains us, brings us together, proximity beyond disagreement, partners in not-knowing. We do not expect to pole vault over ignorance and evade questions. A challenge is to make room for questions in which "I don't know" is essential.

I once had a supervisor who said, "Never ask a question of the patient that you don't know the answer to." What a relief to find workers, like Bion, for whom psychoanalysis itself is a question.

How open can we be, ought we be? Let's not pretend to know ahead of time.

*   *   *

A pointer to infinite openness is the child too simple to ask at the Seder table. The Passover Seder speaks of four children, the wise, the evil, the shy, the simple. When I was a child, I learned that the wise child is interested in everything going on at the Seder table. He asks, "What is all this, this and this?" Everything excites his care and curiosity. He has a hunger for wisdom. He is a good model, who a child should wish to be.

The evil child also asks, "What is all this?" Not in an open spirit but a rejecting one. More like, "What am I doing here? What are any of us doing here? What is all this nonsense?" He represents our closed spirit, our narrowness. Nowadays, he is called rebellious rather than evil. His energy is recognized. Negation has its purpose and potential. But the father's answer in the traditional reading remains the same: "If you were in the land of slavery when God took us out, He would have left you there". Which means the rebellious child has a way to go to free himself from inner constriction: a rebel is a slave once removed. He is a know-it-all in reverse, putting down what is happening without open questioning.

The shy child is too shy to ask. He may want to know but fails to begin the process. He will pick up what he can by watching and hearing what goes on, not without feeling or interest. But his caring is not great enough to break through barriers of personality and initiate outer seeking and searching. He is our introverted side, not without merit. But at the Seder he was presented as deficient, not as open and able as the wise child. We are urged not to hide our ignorance and interest. If you do not know, ask and seek, share not knowing.

The fourth child was simple, perhaps retarded or undeveloped. No ill motives, not wishing he was not there, not hostile. If he felt, "What's going on here?" it was a state of his whole being, his whole being an unaskable question, perhaps a state of bewilderment. Each of these four possibilities represent our own attitudes, each with merits and difficulties. A fifth group not mentioned are all those absent, those who do not show up. In contrast with all present with whatever attitude, they do not bother with the Seder at all. It has lost meaning to them and has become irrelevant. There is much to say about the group that is not there, but that will have to wait for another occasion.

My focus here is the simple child, whom I have come to see as a mystic aspect of self. The wise child is a smarty-pants know-it-all. He follows up on not knowing, wanting to know, asking, but is too goody-goody. I am unfair in using him this way as a foil, as dedicated to K (knowledge) rather than O (infinite unknown), especially when the two are interlaced. But I do so to bring out a vision of the simple child as too overwhelmed to play the knowledge game. He lives in a state of immediate impact, a lightning rod for a mystical dimension of the Seder, lights going off, God-impacts. Like Job, he is driven to silence. What can he say in face of this display, this immensity. Quite a light show. Fireworks do not come near, although they trigger ooohs and aaahs that touch the Great Mystery.

One can call the simple child's experience a kind of knowing, but that scarcely does justice to the awesome, dumbfounding sense of the Infinite Unknown. Knowing lost in being, beyond being. Bion speaks of formlessness as dreadful and creative. But I think the simple child is beyond dualities—and perhaps before. Yet, even in saying this, I make use of a duo, before–beyond.

There is a sense in which the simple child expresses what is permanently embryonic in human nature. All of our life is a birth process, which means we are also ever unborn. Somewhere in his writings, Nicholas Berdyaev describes a neonic dimension, a term that points to a neonatal quality of our beings. He means by this a kind of freedom, presence of possibility. I think, too, of Michelangelo's sculptures called "Prisoners" or "Slaves", in which figures emerge from stone partly formed, partly unformed. The womb-stone from which figures emerge suggests the ever-forming nature of life.

*   *   *

It is said that when right–wrong and plus–minus are mixed, even a Buddha cannot separate them. There are many sayings in Buddhism having to do with cutting out mind and understanding or, as Plotinus says, "Cut away everything". What remains when you cut away everything?

Can I then say, I am here, you are here? We are here! Here is here! Asian artists often resort to poems and drawings of nature at this point. But aren't we miracles too? We are the miracles that give aching expression to miracles of nature, miracles of sight and sound and touch. How to show the miracles we are! Everything we touch bears our imprint. And we bear the imprint of everything we touch.

Returning to the story we started with (p. 32), Katsuki Sekida (2005, p. 148) says that "I don't know" is an inaccurate rendering of Bodhidharma's response to Emperor Wu's question. He feels Bodhidharma's answer should be rendered, "No holiness, no knowing". He goes on to comment that even these terms pile on complications for the Emperor. Why speak of holiness or knowing at all, even if negation of merit and grasping might help the Emperor this moment or in the long run? Inevitable thorns and briars, writes Setcho (*ibid.*, pp. 148–149). A moment calls for response, and one uses what capacity one has.

To dramatize the depth and potency of not knowing, Setcho wrote that even the Ancient Buddhas never arrived and added, "I don't know either" (Cleary & Cleary, 2005, p. 251). Where does the experience of no knowing or not knowing or "I don't know" take you? What does it open? How many of us, how often, and how deeply dwell with this elusive but fecund sense? In childhood, we tease our minds and souls with not knowing who we are or how we got here—anything, everything, the whole universe, life itself, why here, this way? We tease ourselves into oblivion, wonder, and awe and shudder at the discovery of thrills and frights not mentioned by anyone we know, pleasures of going further and further into unknown, nameless whirls, pools within pools, pleasures bottomless, dizzying and unfathomable.

These are pleasures that might be cultivated but rarely are. We learn to coat this secret boundlessness with names, learning, questions, and tasks that aid what we call upbringing and education. In adulthood, some of us, some of the time, search for the missing unknown with impoverished means to engage it. At moments we dip in and begin the great opening. We try and once we taste it earnestly seek more to the extent we dare or can.

How odd it sounds, to seek more of no knowing. To use the very experience of "I don't know" as a gateway to dimensions we are starved for. To go deeper into not knowing who or where we are, and deeper still.

*   *   *

It is said that Buddha reached bottom, the end of it, no more to go, and it is said he never arrived. There is no end to my "I don't know", no bottom. I sit in not knowing with an intimate presence, a close friend, amazing stranger, dreaded power, closer to me than I am. Some say that intimate presence is yourself, your own mind, part of inner dialogue, the broca area, your parents. I do not say no. But something eggs me on, not quite this, not quite that. Nothing I learn about it is quite satisfactory. An amazing presence is embedded in the heart's centre, an infinite, intimate presence. "Who are you?" I ask. Who or what is it? I do not know. Yet, the intimacy of Infinite Intimate Presence is better than "knowing".

If I am pinned to say so, I can be forced to call this a kind of knowing, a special knowing of its own often called a secret knowing. Can I pin this knowing down, know this knowing? To an extent, but in the attempt the deep knowing evades knowing. One can question and pursue *ad infinitum* and come up with useful ideas, visions, science (some claim to be able to locate mystical experience, prayer, and meditative practice in particular brain areas and states). Well and good, but for me there is no substitute for experiencing the deep unknown of this "known". With relief I set aside "knowing" and irritable reaching after facts and reasons, to taste the thing itself. I no longer want to pin it down. I just want to be with it, some might say to be it, although for me it is a presence inexhaustible by myself. I would rather jump in, stay in. The taste is miraculous. It includes the taste of our lives and the indefinable.

*   *   *

I am not at all against the quest to know, curiosity, wonder, knowledge of all kinds. Knowledge feeds survival, up to a point, but is also double-edged, as modern weaponry and toxic side-effects of technical know-how shows. How to use our capacities, all of our capacities, is a great evolutionary challenge.

This is not a discourse against knowing. Without language and cognition and a deep urge to know, how would these words be written? How could I try to communicate with the base of our beings if words did not reach, seep in, make their way to the "bottom" and trigger unknown transformations? Words can touch what most of all counts, and animate and be animated by the latter. Too often, they obfuscate, injure, prevaricate, deform, divert, as can any creative capacity. We have learnt that hell is no barrier to creativity.

The purpose of my words is not to talk against words or the pursuit of knowledge, but to further awareness that there is much to gain from staying with no knowing, "I don't know", not knowing as an experience in its own right, and as a gateway to possibilities of experiencing yet to come. Not knowing is an extremely fecund, vital, and powerful state that can open us in unimaginable ways. The purpose of my words is to get you thinking about what I do not know means to you, and venture in, and keep on venturing. The human race needs to recognize and work with the fact that not knowing is a capacity that is a vital part—a vital centre—of our journey.

* * *

There are practical aspects to not knowing. One, already mentioned, is that it can stimulate learning. Another is that living in unknowing leaves room for other people. Too often, we presume we know who the other is, we know all about him or her, and we become reactive. Our partial knowledge becomes totalized and we saturate the space where another might be. We saturate the mystery of the other with imaginary knowing. I say "imaginary" because acting on partial knowledge as if it is total or more than it is to create a more or less make-believe other, partly real but also partly imaginary. Often, we may not be able to distinguish our make-believe other from the being who confronts us, and our imagination fuels inflammatory reactivity.

Another way of saying this is that we approach another person from the viewpoint of partial omniscience, a sense that what we know is all there is or all we care to know. Many years ago, during the cold war, I wrote of the danger of miscalculation from the viewpoint of omniscience (1986). One side or group or individuals may press a button that releases destruction because they thought they knew something that they did not. The term "pressing a button", in common speech, also refers to hitting emotional nerves. Truth hits emotional nerves but lies do, too. At present, we are living through moments of history where miscalculation from the viewpoint of omniscience has disastrous economic consequences and possibly more than economic. Economic self-glorification and its "righteous omniscience" links with a destructive tendency that hits world nerves. A little not knowing, tempering omniscience, would go a long way.

Not only can not knowing have beneficial effects in relating to others and society, but with oneself as well. The ancient oracle commands, "Know thyself", but imaginary knowing is often a result. Pascal saw that we over and underestimate ourselves, an observation psychoanalysis developed. We oscillate between grandiose and abject states and find these profoundly linked. Scratch one, get the other, a kind of psychic law: live one side, the other comes. In our current day, political–economic–military grandiosity carries devastation in its wake. The two extremes play out across the field of humanity. Processes that wreak havoc in individuals are writ large in society and problems ravaging society are read in the mayhem of individual lives.

Today one is rewarded for knowing who one is, which often means making believe one knows who one is, if not fabricating an identity. We are told, "Follow your dream", as if we should have a dream to follow, a particular target to hit. When I think this phrase through I begin to feel it is too tight for me, something of a straitjacket, and often the goal is over-materialistic and narcissistic. I am hemmed in by "my" dream. I get the feeling I am being marketed to myself, being sold a bill of goods by being funnelled through an "identity". If I am asked "Who are you?" and I give an intelligible answer, I feel that is not it, that is not me—I disappeared as I was speaking.

Even the word dream gets truncated, if not debased, by being turned into a political–economic entity. We are more than the sum of our dreams. At the same time, our dreams may offer us more than we can handle and often try to work with that more. There may be both symmetry and asymmetry in our relations with our dreams or our dreams with us. That is, there is identity and resonance. We share the same concerns and, to some extent, the same space with our dreams. We also differ. Our dreams often rub our noses in what we cannot bear to let in. Sometimes they are bigger than us, sometimes narrower. They can, also, contain experiential germs seeking nourishment and seeking to nourish us.

Psychoanalysis says we are not too good at knowing who we are. We are clowns, often doing things to trip ourselves up. Psychoanalysis tries to tell us certain things it claims we ought to know about ourselves, but the journey continues. Perhaps as important as particular sets of "knowledge" is the methodology of openness it potentially mediates. To be open to not knowing who we are is as important, if not more important, than what we think we know. Bion's reformulation of the psychoanalytic attitude (free-floating attention, free association) as F in O, characterized by eschewing expectation, understanding, desire, or understanding, opens possibilities of transformative living that, by definition, we cannot, now and perhaps ever, grasp. That we cannot understand and think them does not make them less valuable and real.

Bion emphasizes the dread of not knowing, but it is also a relief not to have to know. Is there a God or is there not? Is there life after death or is this it? Who am I? Am I this or am I that? Who are you? Are you who I think you are? How confining would that be?

When I think I do not have to know the answer to these questions, I feel relief. I can breathe more easily. To not have to know what cannot be known. To be as open as one can or dares, intermittently, if not moment to moment. To sample openness throughout a lifetime, as part of the paradoxical mix of capacities we have and are. What a relief not only not having to know, but not pretending to know.

Perhaps we need to practise feeling and saying, "I don't know", like a musician practises scales, as part of an exercise in living. Perhaps we should begin as children. Over time, we may get used to it. Over time, our "I don't know" and us can become friends. From deep not knowing, no one is excluded. We are partners in not knowing and the waiting, caring, sharing it fosters, the patience and sensing needed to live well together, to be intimate with ourselves. How is it possible to be intimate yet unknown, the deeper the unknown, the deeper the intimacy? To enter fields of unknown intimacies opens planes of existence where nothing is required other than to marvel and say thank you. More work comes afterwards.

CHAPTER FOUR

Wordlessness

"There are Buddha-lands where there are no words. In some Buddha-lands ideas are indicated by looking steadily, in others by gestures, in still others by a frown, by a movement of the eyes, by laughing, by yawning, by the clearing of the throat, or by trembling"

(*The Lankavatara Sutra*, quoted in Goddard, 1932)

Wordless reality

These beautiful words touch the possibility of the wordless. Wordless reality. Is there such a thing? For ants, lions, and snakes there is. They get along very well without words, as does most of physical and biological reality. Yet, a case can be made for non-verbal language, chemical signals, bird songs, buzzing of bees, varying "roars" of the lion. Are these, properly speaking, words? Words can make up meanings that refer to things that are not there or do not exist. The Lankavatara Sutra gives as examples, "hare's horns" or "a barren woman's child", words without objects. Animal signals seem to be confined (we think) to what is there or could be there, concerns with pain, pleasure, territory, mating, grief, nutriment, danger, perhaps even songs and gasps expressing awesome surges of beauty.

Some of us argue that words pervade everything. In the beginning was the Word, the creative Word, generator of the kind of life we have and can have. We are born into language. Our body is a language, many languages, and words imprint it. There are many ways to formulate an intimacy between words and life and rupture between words and life. Yet, the value of wordless experience has been affirmed since the beginning of recorded words. Is wordless experience possible with the advent of verbal language? Whether or not it is, it continues to be valued, cared for, mined, touched. One of the great functions of poetry is to find (and create) the thrill of the wordless through words.

*   *   *

The passage from *The Lankavatara Sutra* quoted above (Goddard, 1932, p. 42) speaks of "ideas indicated" by gestures. We are not going to solve or exhaustively study what this might mean (if the passage is tolerably translated). We will play with it a little. If one takes the passage at face value, physical movements indicate ideas. Physical movements have meaning or are not without meaning. This is linked with Buddhist emphasis on mind. Our minds constitute the world we live or the way we live in it, and our minds can be transcended.

There is smaller and larger mind, psychophysical and spiritual reality. More dramatically, in the very next sentence, the *Lankavatara* tells us there are Buddha-lands "transcending words and ideas"; one attains "recognition of all things as un-born".

If we were cognitive therapists, we might emphasize ways that ideas and attitudes, especially affective attitudes, shape experience–behaviour. Ideas imprint body. As a psychoanalyst, I like to say affective attitudes mould body and vice versa.

Read (1957) suggests that image precedes idea by about two hundred years. And before image? Physical gropings, some push from within, experiential pressures, perhaps with a sense of implicit meanings aching for birth. The permanently unborn, aching for birth, giving birth in great variety.

Physical ↔ Mental. When we penetrate either side, we find the other. They are intertwined, one-yet-not-one, not-one-yet-one, a paradoxical monism (Eigen, 1998, forthcoming). We make discriminations like mind–body, without knowing what these names buzz around.

It is like going into a cave and coming out in Wonderland. Or discovering Wonderland, then dropping into shit forever. Alchemists express a fundamental, teleological urge when they try to turn shit into gold. And accidents of language bring us up short with reversible formations like God ↔ dog. Binaries just do not do processes justice, but we lack language and ability to do without them. We try with computer programmes on the one hand, and art and poetry on the other, to express amazing, complex patternings with lives of their own.

We are multitudes of unknown patternings in process, and our minds use concepts as ladles to get a fix on them. Slowly, we learn that conceptual ladles inform us about the ways mind tries to organize reality, ways that mind strains against its limits. And we? It is not unusual to feel boxed in by our minds, our habits, attitudes, sense of self. In older language, we try to push through the prison of ourselves. We try to get out of ourselves, out of our mind.

*   *   *

Some struggle to get into or out of words. The idea of putting feelings into words is an odd locution. How does one do that? Can you picture it? Sometimes I think of drawing feelings from a well and pouring them, a little at a time, into buckets of words. Often we do the reverse. We try to fill the well with words. Instead of drawing from a deep and bottomless well, we pour words into it. We lower word buckets down, hoping to catch something, often coming up with more words. Some of these words are juicy enough, some dry. But we fear that what we pull up is what we put in, missing living water.

Winnicott calls attention to the difficulties wordless people have in a world of words.

> Some babies specialise in thinking, and reach out for words; others specialise in auditory, visual, or other sensuous experience, and in memories and creative imagination of a hallucinatory kind, and

these latter may not reach out for words. There is no question of the one being normal and the other abnormal. Misunderstandings may occur in debate through the fact that one person talking belongs to the thinking and verbalising kind, while another belongs to the kind that hallucinates in the visual and auditory field instead of expressing the self in words. Somehow the word people tend to claim sanity, and those who see visions do not know how to defend their positions when accused of insanity. Logical argument really belongs to the verbalisers. Feeling or a feeling of certainty or truth or "real" belong to the others. [Winnicott, 1992, p. 155]

Differences in sensibility can lead to value judgements about the worth of others, including opinions and definitions of what is real. One source of rancour between people can be rooted in ways they process experience. One can over or undervalue word, vision, and action. Labyrinths of misrecognitions perpetuate themselves in belief systems. When I read a passage like Winnicott's, I feel we are struggling to develop a democracy of voices, a democracy of sensibilities. Winnicott valourizes modes of experiencing and processing experience that are often felt to be mutually exclusive, at war, as if threads of psychic life tyrannize each other. A dominance model goes only so far. A partnership model, emphasizing co-nourishing capacities, needs more room. There are ways, too, that conflict is part of partnership.

*   *   *

I have heard it proposed that silence is needed to process affects. If one talks all the time, one may make discoveries but fail to digest them. They remain momentary flashes. Perhaps someone having such a flash can bring it to fruition Perhaps a moment's flash, then another, and another, is enough. But quiet time is needed to let the flash sink in.

In therapy sessions, I have seen people talk so much they do not hear what they are saying, they do not let it sink in. They speed past the emotional depths of their communications, as if speaking is enough. So many things happen in the speaking. One gets back at others, voices injuries, confesses guilt. Yet, in the speak mode, nothing more may be done, as if saying it is enough, saying it dilutes or gets rid of it or diminishes it enough for the time being.

Letting something sink in and be part of one is something else, something more. Words are an avenue, a conduit, but at a certain point, wordless processing takes over. One is affected through and through but there is a point where the affected self disappears from view. Wordless, imageless being is all that is left. Processing and digestion goes on outside of awareness. The duality being and non-being loses valence, as does the distinction between duality–non-duality.

*   *   *

In the late nineteenth and early twentieth centuries, psychologists investigated consciousness in a number of ways. Areas of interest included judgement and problem solving. Some investigators began to find that at a certain point, usual contents of consciousness faded. Subjects might become hesitant, at a loss, and approach a blank, contentless state, a still point some described as "impalpable awareness". Sometimes a solution to a problem came out of this state, what we might call "out of the blue".

This is not an unusual phenomenon. Gestalt psychology describes moments of impasse, becoming lost in immersion, an imageless, thoughtless absorption, preceding sudden seeing of relations unperceived before, insight into the structure of a situation. In my book, *Flames from the Unconscious: Trauma, Madness and Faith* (2009), I bring out moments of Wittgenstein's and Buddha's experience of deep immersion which open something like psychic wormholes which bring one to new places, experiences valuable in their own right.

Wittgenstein's descriptions of suffering guilt and finding a still point at the bottom of the sea link with Buddha's descriptions of suffering life and awakening. When I read accounts of "impalpable awareness" in graduate school, I felt relief to see academic psychologists come upon states they had no categories for, states that could not be described by sensory content, judgement, thought, image, or will. In 1901, Mayer and Orth and then Marbe (Humphrey, 1948) called various mental events that eluded known categories, *bewusstseinlage*, variously translated as awareness of, knowing that, consciousness or consciousness of, states of consciousness. It could be a kind of intuitive sense of a whole without any clear awareness of details. Or a blank state, a compressed moment, something I might call awarenesses without readily graspable content, sometimes maybe like a hunch or pressure, and sometimes just open and free. Perhaps something like pure awareness, awareness as such.

These states were difficult to describe or beyond description, unknowns. As if consciousness or awareness has a kind of unknown core or that unknowing is one of its "nuclei". The major workers who called attention to this indescribable awareness were part of what was called the Wurzburg school. Their work all but disappeared from the fads and fashions of psychology as it developed but has resonance with certain threads of work today.

Blank consciousness often is associated with psychic depletion, trauma, or psychosis, an impoverishment of psychic capacity (Fliess, 1971). But there is generative blankness as well. I remember a very talkative, angry, stormy patient, Lynn, whom I wrote about in *Reshaping the Self* (1995). At one point, she experienced a sequence of feelings without apparent reason. A flow without thought or image content. I suggested she try to focus on the feelings themselves and just keeping feeling, without trying to figure out why or what, no judgements or interpretations. Stick with the thing itself, as best as possible.

It was like riding bareback without reins. She and the horse had to trust each other. We worked for some time before this happened, so a good deal of therapy faith had the chance to develop, or this kind of psychic hand-holding would not have held. On this occasion, a kind of grace, she let the feelings build and go where they would and stayed with ebbs and flows, now stronger, weaker, fading, returning, like variable volume on a tuner setting itself moment to moment.

In *Reshaping the Self* (1995, pp. 120–123), I spoke of "a wordless self". Self would come, self would go, "self-feeling" waxed and waned. The term sensation is usually reserved for experiences of colour, pleasure, pain, tone, numbness, tingling, etc. It is often distinguished from emotion and feeling. But I find that the latter can be felt, at least partly, as a kind of sensation, too. A feeling sensation. This may include self or no-self sensations, God or no-God sensations, as well as a sensing of a gamut of emotions and dimensions such as empty–full (of life, feeling, lack of feeling). Freud touches this when he calls consciousness a "sense organ" enabling perception of psychical qualities (1900a, p. 51). What kind of sensations are feelings, what kind of sense organ is consciousness?

The first glimmer of Lynn going blank was after she recounted a stormy time with her mother that for years left her not wanting to be a mother. It could have been tempting to interpret the blankness as a response to, or defence against, trauma, a clamming up in face of the unbearable. But that is not what the silent room felt like. There are many kinds of silence and one senses differences. Instead of interpreting in usual ways, I held back and the blankness became a kind of sea or reservoir, positive in itself, a peaceful, refreshing blankness, although it alternated with muted anxiety (1995, p. 73):

> Lynn experienced a fuller sense of what she went through growing up and for some moments was able to relax deeply. Her blankness was alive and resonant before she began to break apart again. For the moment her need to be in control dropped away. On her way out [at the end of the session], Lynn remarked she felt less 'thin.'

Lynn was a regular person trying to live a regular life. Moments of creative stillness are not a prerogative of a creative elite. They are part and parcel of existence, a capacity many have but might not fully tap. It is not so unusual for people to speak of the value of still moments, if given the chance. Some of the most beautiful life experiences involve stillness. Once, in meditation, the words came to me, "unknown intimacies". These words meant intimacies with myself, indescribable and priceless, but not limited to myself. Bion speaks of psychoanalysis as introducing the patient to herself. Such introductions involve history and cognition, but that scarcely taps the profound introduction to the unknown infinite. An infinite that, for Bion, has a psychic primacy.

Many creative geniuses speak of silence, stillness, and related states, often as part of concentration, brewing, intuition, inspiration, or perhaps part of a prolonged impasse. Einstein said he often thought in fragments of images and vague body states, later translating his body "feels" into mathematical and scientific terms. Mozart wrote of a flash, often after a good meal, when he would "hear" or "see" a work all at once without knowing the details. The flash had a certain impalpable feel. These and a rich variety of descriptions of creative moments and processes can be found in Ghiselin (1952).

The flash Mozart describes reminds me of the white flash of *Chochma* in the Sephirot in Kabbalah. The Kabbalah tree has a series of spiritual energy points or psychic organizers that flow from the unknown infinite through Chochma (wisdom) down through other channels (understanding, mercy, judgement . . . action). The flow is both ways, up–down/down–up. Chochma is often described as a flash of white light refracting all psychospiritual colours that make us up and that we partner. If Adam's job was to tend the garden, ours is to tend the garden of soul, our beings, all the amazing capacities we find as we live. Milner (1957, 1987) translates the spiritual to the psychological, exploring flows from up–down/down–up that she frames as consciousness moving into body, body moving into consciousness. Perhaps it is more accurate to say she tends to dissolve artificial dissociations between dualities such as psychological and spiritual, consciousness and body. Dualities break down once you get into details of processes: what is body and consciousness become indistinguishable at certain points. She has many passages linking creativity and silent, ungraspable work in areas of formlessness, elusive to objectifying modes of functioning. States in which physical, psychic, and spiritual awareness work together in interwoven ways. I have written in several places that sensation is ineffable (e.g., 2006), a realization with which I think Milner would agree. She approvingly quotes the poets Thomas Traherne, saying that perception is a form of imagination, and William Blake, saying that perception is infinite.

More Bion

"The fundamental reality is 'infinity', the unknown, the situation for which there is no language—not even one borrowed by the artist or the religious—which gets anywhere near to describing it" (Bion, 1994, p. 372).

The fundamental reality—wordless unknown infinity. No language gets near—anywhere near. Quite an assertion. A strong assertion. Is it an assertion or a confession, an expression of emotional experience, for Bion a fundamental experience? I suspect he is letting us in on a truth about his fundamental experience of life. His words carry not only conviction but reality for me, whatever they mean. I am assuming this statement as background for whatever I write about Bion, although I am moving into other filaments of his thought.

In the nexus of his work, Bion coins the term *alpha function*, and means by it processes that store and digest (or try to digest) emotional experience. As yet unstored and undigested impacts of experience he names *beta elements*. I sometimes describe the latter as impact globs awaiting psychic metabolizing. He calls these impact globs "sensations", but they are not exactly the same as sensations of red, or loud noise, or body thrills, although they may overlap. They are often catastrophic sensations or bits of catastrophe, or intimations of catastrophe. A core catastrophe he has in mind is decimation of the personality, personal catastrophe. One's very personhood is hit, traumatically challenged. He points to what I would like to call a *catastrophic sense*, a *sense* of catastrophe.

Needless to say, a catastrophic sense has a basis in catastrophes that happen in the world we live in, physical and social. Physical blights, wars, economic upheavals, arrays of physical, social, and personal wounds, failure of functioning and the fact of death all feed our sense of disaster (Eigen, 1996, Chapter Sixteen, "Disaster anxiety"). It is a sense that gets transferred to, and perhaps has roots in, the threat of being abandoned by someone one loves or being exploited, misused, abused, suffocated in the attempt to live or live well.

For Bion, the very advent of consciousness, the psyche we have, has a catastrophic element, as if our somatic–psychic being is challenged to support the mind it gives birth to. As if experiencing is too much for the systems we have, too intense, too painful, too vast and fast. Evolution is uneven, producing experiences but not adequate digestive capacities for them, another instance in which production outstrips assimilation, a variation of the unevenness Pascal noticed, always ahead of and behind ourselves.

It belies common sense to think our experience is basically catastrophic. So much in life is good. In the first book of the Bible, God is pleased with his production and feels it basically good. There have been times in my life when I felt it good even in hell. *Jouissance* runs through it, even a *jouissance* of death. Bion's work, however, functions as a marker, a notation, calling attention to a catastrophic sense that is pervasive, that is one of the elements that knits personality together. To overlook the claims of our sense of catastrophe is itself catastrophic.

What is real knocks on the doors of our defences and, if it must, knocks them over, forcing reality upon us. We shut reality out more or less successfully a good deal of the time, and let it in a good deal of the time in well parsed doses. Shutting out and letting in work together, a kind of balance, enabling us to work with what we can as well as we can. But either tendency can go haywire. If shutting out gains the upper hand too much, for too long, reality has to work harder to be noticed and realized. A range of catastrophic events may result, including social and personal warps. Trauma rocks through personality, mind, and society. Helpful inroads to any part of the mix is a start.

Bion's alpha function is meant as an inroad. I attended his seminars in New York City in 1978 when someone asked him, "Why do you create this term, alpha function? Don't we have terms that describe what you mean—primary process, secondary process, others?" Bion responded, "I create a term that has no meaning, a kind of nest where birds of meaning might alight." He wants a fresh start, a new beginning, or, at least, the possibility of a fresh look at how we relate to who we are and what life is. Implicit is the question, "Do we really know what grips us or how? How do we let things in? How do we let our own life in? How do we process and make part of us the reality of our own existence?" The "how" here is not meant mechanistically, but more to stimulate awareness of our reality, our condition, and especially the constitution, organization and movements of emotional nuclei, basic responses to ourselves, to life. The primary "sensations" that need processing are emotional sensations.

Alpha works in many ways, including physical ways. An example of the latter are moments when a ball player makes a terrific catch, a dancer an amazing move, surprising even himself. I would like to call this the flow and rise of power, as if a channel opens, alpha body. Another day or even minutes later, the same player will miss a catch and the dancer feels his legs are cement: beta body. Bion has many passages on body experience and communication, often with an implicit sense that different organ systems have minds of their own (e.g., gut mind, breath mind, sex mind) and that overly dualistic oppositions of body–mind miss realities at stake.

Bion notes that analytic thinking (e.g., Euclidean geometry) and narrative (e.g., dream, myth) can be part of alpha work, but he seems more interested in a third kind of alpha that he does not name. He likens it to reversible perspective and the appearing–disappearing of dream memories (1994, pp. 223–224). Now it is one thing, now another, now it is here, now not. He links this form of alpha, too, with interplay of paranoid–schizoid and depressive positions, alternations of coherence and incoherence. In one passage, he hints at it this way: "alpha-elements cohere, separate, cohere again, separate again, converge, diverge, and so on. It is an experience in which coherence and separation are never observed; at one moment the alpha-elements are coherent and then they are incoherent" (*ibid.*). To say that this alternation is unobserved implies a kind of faith and suggests that what appears as alternation to discriminating awareness may be part of one underlying structure or movement.

In earlier work (1986, Chapter Four, 1992, 1993, 1995, forthcoming), I posited a distinction–union structure, a double tendency in which psychic movements towards distinction and towards union constitute aspects of one structure, a kind of DNA/RNA in every unit of experience. This touches on the kind of alpha work Bion likens to double or reversible perspectives. In several books (1986, 1992, 1995), I traced the function of distinction–union tendencies in clinical work. To see these tendencies with their interweaving and dissociations as currents of a deeper structure adds a degree of richness and wisdom to moment to moment awareness.

Since Bion did not name the kind of alpha we are pointing to here, yet thought it highly significant, I will call it "on–off alpha" as a kind of working notation. It includes the now you see it now you don't, now it's one way, now another quality of experience. I am assuming phenomenological doubleness has unobserved, intricate interweavings, even oneness (there may be many qualities of oneness). This "structure" or "movement" or "state of affairs" has wide application. For example, self–no-self, God–no-God, mind–no-mind, being–non-being, full–empty, distinction–union, samsara–nirvana, attention–no-attention, words–wordless.

Bion touches on a mode of processing that is part of creative work and failure to make room for it contributes to being trapped by false choices and divisions that can degenerate into war between capacities. Cultural history is replete with wars between thinking and feeling, feeling and sensation, one capacity pitted against another in a struggle for primacy. Lopsided struggles to be on top of a hierarchy foreclose awareness of symbiotic interplay, a situation of mutual support and nourishment. It is a situation characteristic of capacities within a single personality and between groups, temperaments and interests in the larger world. Virtually any capacity can function in an alpha and/or beta way, and in anti-alpha ways that damage alpha. The same capacity varies depending on its use, value, and work in a given situation.

Alpha work may be difficult and, in Bion's terms, require suffering experience, including tragic qualities and structures of experience. But too great occlusion of alpha, whether out of need, inertia, or meanness, risks cutting oneself off from vital qualities necessary for existence. The struggle to survive via dominance can become counter-productive. The will to be on top becomes myopic, skewing awareness of larger, contextual realities, for example, undervaluing caring, affiliative tendencies. On–off alpha tries to process both tendencies, since dominance and co-operative caring are parts of larger realities. Look at one, see the other, two attitudes that characterize social life.

How does alpha work? That is a queston Bion keeps open by coining a term like alpha. He gives some hints about methodology. He calls the psychoanalytic attitude Faith, and describes it as being without memory, understanding, expectation, or desire. An attitude of openness, allied to waiting, stillness, requiring patience. He lays it down as an evolutionary challenge, a capacity we need in face of what we do to ourselves in economic, military, familial, and social struggle.

Religious myths and the earliest accounts of history tell us we are menaces to ourselves. Biblical prophets, like many other sages, envision the lion lying down with the lamb, turning swords into ploughs, or, as the prophet Micah puts it, "Do justice, love mercy, and walk humbly with thy God". Their voices try to inject a stream of caring through the social body, where aggressive self-centred tendencies vie with broader co-operative needs. Recognition of both tendencies has a long history.

Murder has been an integral part of social life and, to this moment, we do not know what to do with our murderous beings. The prophets fear the destructive consequences of failure to temper our Numero Uno dispositions. I used to joke that the meek will inherit the earth after the strong kill themselves off. However, things are never so simple. In spite of slaughter in times past, we could not do as much harm to ourselves as we can now, when all parts of the globe affect each other. The amazing systems we have for transmission of information and goods expose us all to each other's schemes, visions, and doings. Some see dominance as a mainspring of survival, others say, give co-operation a chance. We will never stimulate growth of the latter capacity if we do not use it. Like a physical muscle, psychic capacities develop through quality of use.

Similarly, what Bion calls faith, the psychoanalytic attitude, being without memory, expectation, understanding and desire. An impossibility? A necessity? As the Talmud says, we may not complete the task, but we can begin it. Does such an attitude as Bion describes exist? Is it worth cultivating? Practice and see. If Hamlet had truly waited and not simply feigned indecision, he might have broken through the revenge ethic. He might have broken murderous transgenerational chains of transmissions. Can we?

Another thread in Bion's work is Transformations in O, where O is a notation for ultimate reality or perhaps, simply, reality. Reality is a big word and a bigger reality. Reality is everywhere you look. You are reality. It is an amazing gift of the human mind that it can think of being out of reality. It can nullify reality and feel unreal. We can feel unreal and be tormented by living unreal lives. Since there is no way to be unreal, to step out of reality, our unreal lives and its torment are real, too. We are the stunning creatures who can be real–unreal—and we are really both.

A patient came to me and after time together confessed that she felt unreal. Not totally unreal, but like a sliver of light in her chest reaching into her belly, a kind of unreal slit in her being. She does not remember when it got there or when she became aware of it. It became worse in her marriage because she felt life should be real— raising a family, living with a loving man, having her own work. She expected me to talk her out of her sense of unreality, to make it go away. She pictured therapy as the two of us allied against her unreality, finding causes and ameliorating them, turning her into a real person.

She wanted to hear that her sense of unreality was unreal and we could do something about it. Whether or not her wish can come true in the long run, for the moment something in me took the form of validating the realness of her sense of unreality and I found myself saying something like, "What about just feeling it? Just be with it. Maybe taste it, take a look at it, see if it says anything, goes anywhere. Maybe you need time to hang with it, care for it, give it room."

That was not anything anyone ever told her. She was accustomed to running from it, filling it with diversions, shopping, child and house care, details of work, angry flare-ups at her husband, a lot of activity. To make time to feel unreal was counter-intuitive. I was telling her to do what she feared to do, what she could not do. Yet, the idea appealed to her, took her off guard, intrigued her. Perhaps a beginning was not too far away, but it was not any kind of beginning she had pictured.

Were my words part of on–off alpha? A null response to what she posited and presented? I think of Beckett sentences that posit something at the beginning and nullify it at the end. To posit–nullify is a widespread activity on every level, thought, talk, history. Hinduism says Atman is Brahman (I and God are one). Buddhism says why I? Why God? Another field of experience opens. Nullifying is creative. Going beyond positing and nullifying is creative.

Words were involved with my patient. That is the kind of therapy I do, talk therapy. But there were wordless transmissions. An affective attitude was instantaneously transmitted, new for the patient, a sense of making room, staying with, enduring and passing through the taboo against being empty. Word components were important but wordless sensing more so, as an inner barrier began to lift.

Inner sensing might be likened to "inklings", intimations, "feels", overlapping with "unknown intimacies". But the nullifying function can wipe away even these, wipe away even the freeing sense that arises when all is wiped out. What bliss! And even that . . .

How far can we reach? What can one say about Transformations in O? Bion talked and wrote a lot, so does not play down words. Yet words—whatever else they are—are gateways to the wordless. Bion speaks of a "felt need" in us for unconscious processing, including a need to convert conscious experience into dream, a need often "obscured by the analyst's insistence on interpretation of the dream" (1994, p. 184). This is not yet imageless transformation, but it is on the way. There is a Hindu saying that calls what is happening in waking life right now the past, dream life the present, and imageless void the future. Even in dreams there are holes, openings, caesuras, blank spots, the thrill of the void.

So much transformational work goes on in reality deeper than dream. Now and then we get inklings of this transformational work, hunches, intimations that bubble up into consciousness as fear, appreciation, or questions. In a way, Bion sees verbal thought and statements as questions (1994, pp. 190–191, 192–197). Words are existential questions. They express experiences that echo on all levels of our beings, whether in the form of silence, waiting, hearing God in the stillness, tasting our own realness in hidden or less hidden ways, expressions of awe, generosity, or thoughtful scrutiny from poetry to mathematics. Our life is a question to life. Also, an exclamation point!

Bion speaks of the analytic session as a special time and goes so far as to call it "the only time when I can have contact with what I do not know" (1994, p. 214). Contact with what is not known is the ground of the session, a sense that runs through it that supports what is said and talked about. That the session by its reality models contact with what is not known may be a source of fear of psychoanalysis. There is so much pressure in public life to act as if one knows more than one does, or even believe one knows what one thinks one knows. An enterprise like psychoanalysis, grounded in unknowing, seems an odd beast indeed.

Psychoanalysis turns things upside down, grounding itself in what is not known, resisting the pull of certainty or fancying one knows more than one does. With various strokes of his brush, Bion links Socratic ignorance, faith as a gesture towards the unknowable, and various eastern and western moments of opening. F in O links with T in O. Wordless, imageless faith in unknowable reality and wordless, imageless transformations that go on in reality. The various systems of thought, social life, orientations, and belief grow like arrays of colourful animals and flowers from largely creative processes we know or suspect we know or imagine we know bits of. One translation of Ayin Soph, the infinite unknown God of Kabbalah, might be infinite nothing. A song that ends many Jewish services says of God, "there is none else", there is nothing but God. This nothing, which we sometimes think of as creativity itself (without reaching towards distinctions between creation and destruction) remains a mystery. We try to water reality down to make it handleable. But some of us, some of the time, and some of us more of the time, develop a taste for the mystery itself and all that reality does without our knowing. How do we appreciate it without the capacity to know? By that special sense no one has yet exhausted and that has called so may forms of expression into being as testimony, as partner, to share and take forward.

Faith is rooted in the unknown, if it can be said to have roots. Whether it is an unknowable God or a state of affairs ever receding from the knowledge quest. Buddhism claims experience of ultimate reality, a kind of knowledge allied with wisdom. In psychoanalysis, this experience beyond experience is real too. Faith, also, is a theme in Buddhist literature, whether a methodological faith that keeps the practitioner on a path yet to be discovered and fully lived, or in the goal region itself, which links with an attitude of sincerity, compassion, a faith-ful life. There is a state where K and F are not distinguishable, at once co-nourishing and coincident. In everyday life, they balance and question and stimulate each other, although dissociated extremes can wreak social and personal havoc. There are, also, states that nothing can describe, that faith and knowing touch, brush, taste, then throw up their hands, stop being tortured and torturing, and let wordless work go on by itself.

CHAPTER FIVE

Ring–hang up, start–stop, on–off

A colleague tells me her patient rings the phone and hangs up over and over. Ring–hang up, ring–hang up. This happens at unexpected times, often at night, not too late as to break into sleep, but almost.

My colleague (C) is, needless to say, exasperated. She has almost lost her sense of wonder. She has no idea what this is about or has many ideas, but they are only ideas, so amount to no idea at all. From a point of frustration, she imagines the patient is hostile or is being prurient, interrupting late night activity (how many little children would like to join their parents in late night play?).

It did not occur to her that the ring–hang rhythm *was a rhythm*, a kind of start–stop, towards–away rhythm, perhaps part of a deeper rhythm that characterized her patient's life. Frustration saturates imagination.

The word hang (as in hanging up) is a bit ominous and teasing: to leave one hanging, swinging on a rope or hanging by a thread (threat?). What is it P wanted C to get the hang of or what did P want to get the hang of? I think of people who from an early age had their feelings aroused and dropped. One scenario is a parent who needs to get the baby or child into an excited state, only to turn off. A pattern of heightened arousal is followed by dropping off a cliff. Emotionally, one is not even left hanging. Cold water is poured on hot emotion and the flame is put out. Start–stop, on–off. It is a scenario that occurs in therapy, too. A therapist may cultivate a patient's dependency, then emotionally disappear. Therapy often reconstitutes family trauma, hopefully with the ability to go through it with some gain.

P's ring–hang rhythm could be a condensed synopsis of a story of her life, highlighting something gone amiss with the capacity to make–break contact. Activities like peek-a-boo and hide-and-seek practise being lost and found, here and gone, seen and unseen, and have to do with affect rising and falling, filling–emptying. Maybe P was practising something akin to feelings–no-feelings, there–not there. Where is the patient? Where is the therapist? Where are the feelings?

Within three months of our discussion, the calls stopped. I do not know why. Did our discussion help take the edge off C's helplessness and open a more curious, embracing space? Was she more appreciative of P needing to constitute a sense of missed meeting that goes on and on, a forever almost that has impact? My guess is C felt less straitjacketed by the situation and more able to absorb the message and communicate that the transmission was received.

A colleague from another country referred a patient to me who called but did not leave a message I understood. I tried to decipher the number he left but when I called back the number did not work. This happened several more times over the next weeks. I was able to understand his English, but the number he left was unreachable. Did I keep mis-hearing? I dialled possible combinations. Did he keep leaving a wrong number? This continued for two or three months and I was about to give up. Finally, the referring colleague contacted me and I told him of my frustration on not being able to reach this patient. I told him I was on the verge of signing off. My colleague said, "If he didn't have a communication problem, he wouldn't be calling for help."

My colleague's remark released me and I felt more open again. It was a mini-sartori: of course! The communication difficulty was part of why this person sought help! The next time my colleague's referral left his number, I was able to get through, and we worked well together for several years, until life took him back to his homeland.

I remember, fifty years ago as a young therapist working with schizophrenic children, telling my supervisor about mounting frustration and anger. One of the children was driving me especially crazy and I was on the verge of blowing. I got tighter and tighter. In "therapy language" of the time, I spoke of the child's "resistance", meaning resistance to getting helped by *me*. My supervisor did not blink an eye and said with instant immediacy, "You're talking about *your* resistance to *him*. It's *your* resistance he's feeling!" I felt a moment's resentment, then, pop: of course! Was it true? It was worth a try. The job became me working on my attitude, a work that continues to this moment, although reminders are needed.

The last of the phone communications I wish to share has to do with a woman referred by two colleagues as "untreatable". The moment I saw her I liked her. She seemed so in the open, like a little animal caught by a spotlight at night in a clearing, so uncovered. It was something about her skin, thin, light, transparent. It gave new meaning to the phrase, "thin-skinned", almost no skin, yet translucent, shimmering like a barely visibly shaking leaf, a nearly imperceptible tremolo. She was very sensitive and more than very intelligent, brilliant, cutting. I felt she could cut through anything except her own depression.

She was a very depressed woman on much medication for many years, perhaps all her adult life. At this point, her psychiatrists did little except adjust dosage or vary medications now and then. Most of the time she used what she felt she needed and took care of herself—barely. She was always on the edge, although I cannot say what she was on the edge of—dying? fading out? sinking to oblivion? going to bed and never getting up? becoming comatose while alive?

Yet, she functioned. Most of the time she went to work and did well. She had a responsible position requiring judgement and brains. After work, she went home, took to bed and faded into hinterlands between living and dying. I could see why she was a scary patient and I was not immune. I do not know any therapist who would be happy if a patient committed suicide. Already I could feel my mind grasp for rationalizations, thinking things like if she killed herself on my watch it could have happened with any therapist and was simply the luck of the draw that it fell on me. Yet, from the instant I saw her I felt she would live. She was a survivor. She would not pull a Hemingway or a Sylvia Plath. She was used to depression. It was where she lived. She would see life through.

We persisted on the edge for two years. I did the best I could but knew it was not enough. It was difficult to admit that my colleagues were right about her being untreatable. I am not sure what happened at the end. She liked talking with me and I liked talking with her. For someone who spent so much time alone and in bed, she knew a lot about a lot of things. She felt some sense of support from our visits, then stopped coming. She ran through whatever it was that made her come for a while and went on alone, back to the life she knew and lived.

About a month later I received an angry call from one of her past therapists about his unpaid bills. She owed him money and ignored his calls and bills. I personally liked this therapist but felt it odd to be called about his bills. I never had a problem with this patient's bills, which she always paid in a timely fashion. I felt funny being put in an in-between position, commiserated, but told him I could not help him. I recognized we had different feelings for this woman. Why I liked and appreciated her and he was so angry I did not know. Maybe he is more honest? Or perhaps we tuned in to different aspects of her personality?

Several months after this call I got another from the same therapist, who began by saying, "I'm so sorry." He went on to say he had learnt that my patient killed herself and he was commiserating with me about this terrible outcome. I was dumbfounded and my insides fell through the floor. I felt awful, yet something grew in me that could not believe it. Her old therapist said he found out about it when the latest of his bills came back marked "Deceased". After hanging up, a sense of being baffled mounted, but I felt horrible. Later that week, in the middle of the night, I awoke with an apodictic sense, clear as light: "She's alive!" It happened just like that, cutting the fog.

It took these several days to link up with another of my first reactions to his call, which had been suppressed: "I don't believe it." I could now remember that along with going through the floor and feeling horrified, a sense of disbelief came up and was shunted aside. I could not suppress a smile of relief and also a laugh at realizing she had played a "joke" on my colleague.

In the morning I called her apartment. Someone picked up the phone, hung it up after I said hello. A few minutes later my phone rings and the caller hangs up after I answer. She let me know she was all right and that she stiffed my colleague.

I sat in a soft peace, an inside smile at twists and turns of life, the forms of communication that are possible. I was relieved to know she was all right. Yet, something in me already knew. I felt something between us through this ring–hang up transmission. The time we spent together was worthwhile. We made some kind of contact, cared for each other and shared a comic view of the universe in deeply tragic places. It was a moment with ripples I feel today.

Start and stop: a Bion case

Bion's clinical portrayals often illustrate what I am calling a start–stop (ring–hang up) tendency. The case focused on here is in a section of *Cogitations* (1994, pp. 218–221) called "The analyst's Odyssey".

Bion begins: "The patient comes to the door and looks away . . ." These are the first words of his clinical description. The patient comes to the door. That already is an achievement for a "psychotic" patient, for many patients (Bion's work is deeply concerned with psychosis, psychotic states, and psychotic attitudes in individuals and society). To actually come to therapy, to seek therapy, find a therapist, come and come again and keep coming—for many people, this does not happen. There are many who do not seek the help they need, or cannot make use of it, or leave before they are helped. We are already ahead of the game with this patient. He comes and keeps on coming.

He comes and looks away. He comes but breaks contact, does not let it build. Coming is all he can manage for the moment. To make more contact is too much. He/his body find ways to be there without overloading himself. To show up and make eye contact in one sequence is more than he can bear. The patient has found ways to modulate his sensitivity to contact, going towards–away so that he is not overly stressed. He may or may not have looked away "on purpose". It may be something like a reflex, automatically pulling back so that too much does not happen. A measure of safety is preserved.

My guess is that toning down the stimulation enables him to take the next step and actually enter the office. Looking away conveys the message not to expect too much, not to make any great demand. One might say that it partly obliterates the analyst, treats him as if he is not there. There may be truth to that, but it is also likely that he partly blots the analyst out so that he can sustain being there at all. In this instance, breaking contact is a way of allowing whatever bit of contact is endurable.

A lot happens in the first moments, but one can already discern a pattern of starting–stopping, going towards and pulling back. Bion's patient offers his hand to be shaken but it is limp. He begins to speak, then says he does not have much to say. His gloves do not match. He is unkempt and dirty, as though semi-lack of self-care ensures sufficient distance without making him impossible to be with. Tension rises, he feels anxious, then looks at one of his hands and follows its movement as if it were someone else's, or a hallucination. Tension ebbs, he folds his hands on his chest in a rest-in-peace position, ready to sleep.

Bion uses the term constant conjunction for images or actions that appear together with some reliability. Like ringing the doorbell–looking away; speaking–fading out; a sense of tension, pain rising, then dissipating and blanking out. A conjunction of tension and detachment, as if hints of pain or potential pain go with not being there, abstracting oneself from the situation, dissociating from what one might feel. This conjoining of tendencies—to feel and not feel, or almost feel and almost not feel—becomes something like second nature, a chronic state of affairs, a "habit" sequence that runs off by itself.

Bion notes that his patient's "face almost expresses physical pain." (p. 218) Then describes tension in his patient's body that the latter hallucinates away. A little later, Bion moves in his chair and his patient "starts violently, as if I had frightened him beyond endurance, or maybe even struck him. His attitude expresses intense pain".

Acute sensitivity coupled with blunting; momentary heightened arousal together with readiness to subside. It is as if his patient's psyche–body are in a chronic spasm. Self-gripping, knotted, self-strangulated coupled with going limp, dropping away. The startle response—almost mimicking acute pain—refers back to acutely painful shock moments without defence or resources which, over time, underwent deadening. The body becomes a graveyard for insoluble pain, its tension an armour, an alarm, chronically blotting out emotional–somatic memory of pain without end.

Again, the patient tries to speak. "There is something I meant to say." Then peters out. My sense is that there *was* something he meant to say, something his being, his psyche needed to say, something about the truth of his life, what it is like being him. But the trauma of existence could not be said. Bits of it could be shown in fragmentary, truncated ways. We feel the strangulated state of his existence.

A picture emerges of psychosomatic tension rising and falling around nuclei of pain expressed indirectly by body gestures and verbal fragments with their desultory, aborted fate and timing. The life or truth of the session was an aborted psyche, an aborted body, an aborted birth.

In another session, the patient speaks of people "cutting the grass", "the tea was awful, really awful", "no home, tea all over the place, I simply will not stand it". Bion comments that the last words were said "with a kind of desperation, as if he were attempting to break through a restraining barrier formed by an inability to express himself in terms that would link him with another person" (p. 219).

Cutting refers to traumatic pain. There are colloquial phrases referring to being cut down, cutting remarks, cut out, part of a language of injury. Freud called attention to this linguistic stream when he wrote that words or looks can feel like "a blow to the face" or "stab in the heart". He remarked that this is not simply metaphorical, but refers to real emotional pain with possible somatic consequences.

Bion's patient uses a spasmodic language of injury to refer to emotional pain and failure of emotional nourishment: cut, awful taste, no home. "I will not stand it" also implies that he cannot stand it. He tries to encompass incapacity in an image of will. He cannot stand the pain of existence, cuts, emotional homelessness, the awful taste of his life. Bion deepens our sense of incapacity by adding that it is not simply incapacity to bear the pain of injury, but inability to break through a barrier formed by difficulty in finding a way to communicate one's pain to another, hopeless futility in the process of communication. One's attempts at communication exacerbate the injury one tries to relieve. Despair, futile fury, cutting off and turning off result from aborted or damaged ability to link in a fuller way with one's feelings, with oneself, with another. Perhaps a sense of not being able to stand it functions as a link, an *I can't stand it link*, expressing and dampening unendurable pain, indirectly, many times removed.

In still another session, Bion's patient recounts an episode (real, imagined, hallucinated?) in which a waitress makes him wait and he becomes furious. "I just broke the place up . . . oh, shut up. *Shut up*, I say. Shut *up* . . . I must have done something wrong." The patient trails on, saying the session is wasted, that he had something very important to say and ends by saying and whispering, "Shut up, shut up."

Some constant conjunctions in the session: furious–shut up and important–wasted. Maximum–minimum emotion. One feels the shut up through one's psyche, one's body, one's being. It is akin to screaming, "Get away! Get away!" Freud speaks of flooding as primal trauma, too much feeling, intensity, and stimulation. A need to turn down the volume and, if necessary, shut it out. The problem with shutting out one's feelings is that one shuts oneself out as well.

Who or what is this blanket shut up addressed to? The waitress (mother, source of care and nourishment)? Analyst? Or, more deeply, the patient's own self? A shut up that runs through the fury of existence. One feels a body gripping, holding tightly, rings of tension stiffening life.

At the centre is *something wrong* (see "Something wrong" in *Flames From the Unconscious: Trauma, Madness, and Faith*, 2009). Something wrong runs through the feel of the patient's life. A mute sense of something wrong, a chronic, frozen scream at the heart of Bion's portrayal. A soundless scream that *is* the session (Bion, 1970, Chapter 2; Eigen, "Screaming" in *Rage*, 2002).

Bion speaks of his own frustration. Nothing he says seems to make a difference. One is driven to the conclusion that frustration itself is part of an emotion the patient is communicating and Bion passes it on to us. Frustration as a link. As Bion puts it, he is forced to have an emotional experience he cannot comprehend and cannot learn from it. Part of the experience is precisely an apparent lack of change and learning, although it seems to me that learning to be with such an experience is already on the edge of learning. We are learning to be with experiences in which learning does not seem possible.

Near the end of his seminars in New York City (1978), Bion remarked, "At least you know what it feels like to have a patient like me." He conveyed the importance of sticking with a sense of difficulty. And with the patient above, sticking with a sense of lack of getting anywhere and the emotional wall that is transmitted. At the end of the New York seminar, Bion said something like, "Funny what pleasure there is in going through something like this, our time together." And near the end of the clinical vignette focused on here, he writes, "What in fact links us is endurance, fortitude, patience, anger, sympathy, love" (p. 220). I suspect what he means includes everything the patient and analyst go through together. If at the centre is frustration, it is a frustration with many colours, a frustration that binds over years. And Bion confesses that in the heart of that frustration is love.

Bion notes that much of what the patient says can be heard as comments on what links them, the link of banging their heads against walls together. "Something wrong" is part of their relationship, the workshop they create together, a Petri dish in which they stare at life's pain together, and keep on staring, a living with, a living through. Bion firmly conveys that something stifles existence and, without naming or stifling it, he opens a space for what stifles us.

Another patient cannot stop talking, a flood of disjointed phrases, names. Bion writes, "The essential feeling is that nothing can be made of it" (p. 221). Yet, Bion did make something of it. He summarized the man's disjointed flood as cries of, "Help! Help! I'm drowning, not waving."

"Help! Help! I'm drowning, not waving." The essential communication is pain that has undergone much deformation, rerouting, covering, yet survives in the patient's body as spasm, language as spasm. A kind of gripping on to words as rafts in the flood. A stalemate, as words are part of the flood. Emotional pain frozen in the body, in language. Body and words as fossilized injury. Psychotic communication may contain hints of deep meaning, but it is also an

SOS, a depleted shriek the subject no longer accesses, but which accesses him. Patient and analyst at the edge of stalemate. Enduring together brings new capacities into play.

On–off experiencing

Bion notes several ways of attempting to record and process experience. Two are familiar: narrative sequences as in dreams and logical connections and analysis as in Euclidean geometry (p. 224). He describes a third mode of experiencing and processing experience that is not so familiar, which I call on–off thinking or feeling or experiencing. He tries to give us a sense of it by comparing it to reversible perspective, for example, seeing a beautiful woman in a picture one moment, a skeleton the next. As one looks, what one sees changes and changes again. Now it is this, now that. He likens this, too, to remembering a dream one moment, its disappearing the next. Or, again, elements of experiencing cohering, separating, cohering, separating. Now x is here, now y, different patterns of organization, different experiential possibilities.

It is a mode of processing with wide application. For example, self–no-self, emptiness–plenitude, form–formless, nirvana–samsara, here–gone, unite–untie, God–no-God. As if the mind or psyche has a blinking activity, open–close, now you see it, now you don't. Disappearance is implicit in experiencing what appears and vice versa, parts of a creative rhythm.

In this process, something may seem to come out of nowhere, akin to lightning-like processing of life, a flash, an intuition. Such words are leaden compared to the moment itself. One needs to grow into the on–off rhythm of experiencing, make room for it.

One's own being may flicker, now more a sense of being, now less, towards on, towards off. At times, the flicker is very slow, imperceptible, but hints of it may arise. Many psychotic individuals, when therapy reaches a certain point, dream of corpses coming alive. As the corpse shows signs of life its bones or limbs begin to move slowly and creakingly. Creaking is audible in the dream and almost audible in the hearing of the dream. Rusty bones, beginning to move. One feels it as the patient tells it. A taste of on–off life–death rhythm begins to emerge.

To study this form of thinking, feeling, experiencing, being is a worthwhile project in itself. Here, I only note its existence and importance for the cases I have touched on here. All the cases demonstrated a start–stop tendency. Often the start–stop, on–off rhythm was stuck, frozen, rigid. Not entirely stuck, as movement over time developed.

I picked examples with ring–hang up as it seems a vivid image of reaching out and not being able to sustain reaching out. Hello–goodbye. Not even hello: ring–hang up. It is a process more widespread than imagined. It grips the body, the psyche, and the social body. Something beginning (a feeling, a thought, sensation, intuition, project, relationship), and stopping, turning off, psychically disappearing. A stop–start, here–gone rhythm is part of creative living. What would it mean to traverse the whole arc of an experience and see it through, stop–start/on–off processes gone through many, many times? It would take a kind of growing into the experience, growing with it, making room for it and oneself. Growth of a sense of the start–stop/on–off quality of experiential movement. Very like growing with a family as it grows/fails to grow or staying with a work of art or relationship as it opens–closes, flickers on–off. Only here the work is staying with one's own unfolding as it flickers on and off.

Bion's examples are acute portrayals of the on–off rhythm gone wrong, stuck, in ways stillborn, as though the personality settled into more or less ossified patterns of staying a little alive while denuding itself of life. Any rise of feeling meets the great "Shut up!" As the volume of life rises, it elicits a signal to turn off. Life on–life off. Hints of life on–hints of life off. Still, a nucleus of life comes through the stillbirth of therapy: "Help! Help! I'm drowning . . ."

"Help! Help! I'm drowning . . ." This is a message that comes through loud and clear, a still, small voice from the frozen whirlwind. Therapy as an SOS. Raw life struggling to live, no matter how suffocated, deadened. Bion gets it and shares it with us. Not that he or we have a solution, no one size fits all. But at least we have a better sense of what we are up against and perhaps even allow our own on–off experiencing to come into play. Our own birth is at stake in every therapy, living and learning more about being–vanishing from moment to moment and over time.

CHAPTER SIX

Tears of pain and beauty: mixed voices

K urt was ambivalent about coming into my office. His hesi-
tancy showed up in his difficulty making an appointment.
For several months he called and hung up, then left
messages I could not quite understand and phone numbers that did
not work. Finally, by some act of grace or a happy click of a psychic
slot machine, we made contact.

Ten minutes past our appointment time, I found him standing
outside my door when I went to check the mail. He could not bring
himself to walk in or ring. He knew from our phone contact that I
leave the outer door unlocked and that he could come in to the
waiting room. He could not say why he was standing there,
whether he was paralysed, wanting to be there and not wanting to,
tempted to run away, dash out of the building and on to the street,
where he felt safe. For him, walking the streets meant freedom.

When he came in he looked at me sternly and repeated over and
over: "The simplest kind of proposition, an elementary proposition,
asserts the existence of a state of affairs."

"You are here," I proposed. I was thinking perhaps this was an
elementary proposition asserting the existence of a state of affairs,
although I was not sure. I recognized his words as a quote from

Wittgenstein's *Tractatus* and something in me translated it into a probe of existence, his existence. My mind conjured that he was seeking and feared some kind of elemental contact, dread and hunger for elementary contact with himself and that I was here to help mediate that contact. I also was aware of my thoughts as a psychoanalytic fantasy.

Later I learnt that saying "You are here" was both threatening and relieving. To be here meant not to be on the streets. To be here with someone, potentially suffocating. There is no question that he pictured therapy as violation, robbing him of himself. Through my blinds he could see slits of street life, slivers of people walking by, street noise, traffic, voices, children and parents, one way cell phone conversations passing, sunlight and shadows. Life outside the window comforted him.

"You know what it's like for me to be here," he said quietly. We stood looking at each other. His eyes seemed to focus on me intently as if I were the bulls-eye of a target, yet darted around, not landing anywhere, looking at everything out of the corner of his eye, not wanting to be trapped by anything.

"You know I can't be here." He sounded on the verge of tears, then turned and looked at the door. Was he going to rush out? Going into my office and sitting down felt like caging a lion. I was motionless.

He saw the door to the inner room, the consulting room, and slightly bent toward it. I bent with him.

"Thank you," he said.

*   *   *

A month later he said (speaking of our first moments of meeting), "I was impressed you knew the Wittgenstein quote and said nothing about it. You pointed out I was here, proposition in action, beyond proposition. You let me off the hook. You didn't rub my nose in anything, not those first moments. You let me escape. That enabled me to come in. I felt I could get out and felt that you felt I could. How *here* I can be remains to be seen. I suppose you feel that way about yourself, too."

I tend to cut things off, bolt. Like Kurt, I am sensitive to suffocation. But I can be pretty sticky, too. If I bolt, I come back, stick to it, a minute later, an hour or week later, whatever it takes to recuperate and regroup. Therapy with Kurt might end today or tomorrow or go on for years and years. Opposite tendencies go together. No way to know how we might navigate them.

It is not easy to be with another person or to be alone. Many bolt from themselves, fear their own stickiness, fear being stuck with themselves. After being lost in thought, words bubbled out of my mouth like captions in a comic book, the kind in which tragic guts of characters smear the page: "It's a challenge to stay in the same room together and a challenge to stay in the same room with oneself as well."

He knew what I meant, the endless sense of being stuck. Wherever he is, wherever I am—stuck. Stuck with ourselves, the unsolvable problem of ourselves. He added, "I didn't know it was like this everywhere. On the street it's not there. You walk and walk and look and look. You don't have to be anywhere with anyone. You don't have to be anything at all. Just walk and look." You walk yourself out, walk out of yourself, into yourself, through yourself. An area of freedom. But stuck comes again.

"Being somewhere with someone is too hard for me," he continued. He might have added that being somewhere with himself is too hard, too. "There's a hell in me and walking is like pouring water on a fire. The fire doesn't go out but the water feels good while it's there."

I did not rub his nose in the fact that we were talking, making contact with our insides, letting each other know. Our contact may be fragile, yet the need for psyche talk is strong. Much more important than glomming on to little signs of "improvement".

* * *

Kurt was in his early thirties and had been hospitalized three times. He saw evil spirits in people's expressions that terrified him. Not all people, but mostly those close to him and others as well. A voice within told him to flee and not think where he would go. He would be told when the time came. The important thing was to get away, go, go, go.

This was a test of faith. If he could not do this it meant he lacked faith and was condemned to unspecified eternal doom. Salvation lay in his hands, if only he would listen to the voice and escape. If only he had the courage.

Sometimes, these urges were laced with vague murmurings of Lot escaping Sodom, or Orpheus Hades. DON'T LOOK BACK. GOGOGO. The voice that whispered commands was the true one and only Way. What paralysed Kurt was not so much another voice, but fear. Blind fear for survival. He imagined if he followed the command all the way he would die, run over by a car or train, shot by a policeman. He would plunge to his death, a cliff, subway track, window. To remain alive meant he was a coward. He dared not take the leap into the True Path.

My mind perceived vast tangles, too early to mention aloud. Perhaps we would never talk about them. Maybe they are intellectual exercises and reality is something else. My mind quickly ran ahead, tying, untying knots, switching switches, a kind of manic assault on psychosis. One madness pursuing another.

Here is what I saw. To leap into the True Path to his death might be a kind of psychological–spiritual "death", part of a transformational process, a "rebirth" process. A problem in psychosis is that commands are taken "literally". You must do this, must not do that. They could not be taken as invitations to change, messages, or announcements: more exists, more is on the way. There is more to you than you know, more to life that you are living. It is hard, if next to impossible, to re-shift the pull, the centre of gravity. The commands stick with unimpeachable authority. One is judged by them. If one does not follow them one is doomed, lacks courage, lacks faith, lacks the courage of one's faith. There are no shades, no continuum, no variation through which one mutates. One is stuck with the judgment and paralysed by the need to survive. One is rendered profoundly immobile, no matter how fast the flight of ideas.

Another thread in the tangle is that the death feared has already happened. One is caught between catastrophe that will befall one if one does not follow the commands and catastrophe that will befall one if one does. In my psychoanalytic vision or fantasy, I sense a catastrophic process at work in Kurt's life, perhaps from early years, ongoing now, and threatening to gather more momentum in the future. His life and personality as harbouring catastrophic dimensions is given expression in the catastrophic dreads that assail him. Psychosis is a catastrophic process. And the sensed catastrophe is given expression in thought and image (delusions, hallucinations).

Catastrophic roots are unknown, whether physical, emotional, environmental, or all combined. But the result is an emotional catastrophe of grand proportions. An upheaval of the I, the sense of self, the ground one stands on. The ground opens and swallows one, but one returns. Over and over. How to make the return fruitful, a growth experience, a creative happening. Is it possible? Not for everyone, perhaps. But some come back and testify, there is life after psychosis. It is possible to return from decimation and enter larger areas of life. Part of the process is little by little, over time, making room for catastrophic processes. So that, in the long run, with much work and help, there are ways that psychotic catastrophe need not be so disabling or that catastrophic processes, in adumbrated form, become part of a larger life.

A third part of the tangle is the mix-up of voices. A voice that claims to be God's may be the Devil's and vice versa. There is profound confusion of voices with no way to tell the difference. One thinks one is commanded by God to drop everything and go, but Satan may be in the mix. And the fear for survival may be a blessing of the body, a touch of sanity. In this case, the urge to survive gets put down by the devilgod, the God–Devil fusion. A sense of life gets condemned if it does not follow Authority (the devilgod, goddevil). What is most sane about one—the urge to survive—gets condemned. In Kurt's case, his walking, sensing. For in his walking he saw colours, smelled scents, felt breezes through his skin, felt the inside good feeling of body movements in cells, tissues, pores, felt alive. And it was the very goodness of feeling alive that was assailed by the demonic, godly commands, masquerading as "The Truth". The tyranny of "truth".

A fourth tangle is possibly even more ominous and unyielding. To be caught between the urge to survive and following The Truth. Either one can be tyrannous, murderous. The fear for survival can drive one to lie, cheat, injure, kill. To do what one needs to do to stay alive at almost any cost, no matter what deformations one undergoes or wounds one inflicts on oneself and others. Fear for survival need not drive one to ultimate extremities, but it may, as witnessed by wars between nations, crime on the street, and business "killings" in high and low finance. One is caught between crazy command structures that drive one to death and fear for survival that deforms one's existence. What is an answer to this knot? At the moment, make room for it, see it, feel it, taste it. Our attempts to solve or escape from it often draw the noose tighter.

It is unclear what my meditation on "tangles" contributes, since my thinking–envisioning does not "solve" anything, does not make problems or torment go away. Still, whether right or wrong, whether used explicitly or not, psychic cud chewing forms part of the background feel of what I bring to the room. I may or may not have the details right. But such reveries carry emotional weight in that they embody concern for a catastrophic impasse that Kurt lives, a tragic impasse. They contribute to an empathic background, appreciation of difficulty, a modicum of a shared sense of pain and quandary, ongoing wondering about what it is we are caught in.

*   *   *

Three years later

"I found a job on Craig's list, helping with sets on a small movie production. I mostly follow orders but help solve small problems too, building, repairing, rearranging. I love it. It's a team, everyone contributes. We do what we can, what we're there for. What I especially like is disagreements and how they get resolved or lived with. There are flare-ups, then you can see a person thinking things through again from another perspective, looking at it this way, that way, seeing what works. The whole thing is about what works. You pour your ideas in the pot with everyone else's and they cook.

"I couldn't do what you do, sit in one spot all day. I like to move. The word "movie"—I feel happy not being still. Movies move. Time moves. The movie is about change, what changes, what doesn't. Characters are moved by life and move us into life. We feel life. We move with them. I can sit still and watch a movie. Movies fascinate me. You can stop a frame and see expressions closely like you can't in real life. You can't get as close to a person as you want and look and look. Face is a sea, ripples, waves. Expressions keep changing, little changes moment to moment.

"It's not a matter of pinning them down, stopping the motion in a still frame. It's more a matter of opening the face up, seeing what's there by slowing it down. To gaze and gaze. It never stops, like slow changes of a sunset. Movies alert you, raise your consciousness to what is there, what *can* be there.

"Someday I'd like to make a movie. Maybe more than one, maybe a lot if I can. I don't know if I can because I get stuck in small frames, tiny bits, curls of lips, frown ripples, glimmers of mouth. I'd have to break off and not fall through a moment or I'd never get to the next moment. I'd have to start all over. Which is ridiculous— next moments keep coming. You focus on what is happening but it's the future coming. You're really looking at the future.

"A gap between the past and future feels so sad. So sad in a mellow way. Sadness that makes you feel it's all right because it isn't. It sticks in your throat, in your chest. You bite the apple of time. You swallow it. It swallows you. Wallow in swallow. I want to say something more, something that can't be swallowed easily, that pierces time."

We have come a long way in three years. Kurt has not closed up, has not been hospitalized, is no longer on medicine. It is still too early to be sure, but we are on the way. Aspects of his psychotic states seem to be channelled into creative work and ability to express himself, his visions, his feel for things. The conduit between sanity and madness has not been closed off. Flow between different levels of being is part of his aliveness.

Glimpses of the first three years out of hospital

At first, Kurt spent a lot of time alone. He would walk through the city, the parks, by the rivers. Often he would find a place in the park and sit for hours, watching, listening, eyes closed, eyes open. Sometimes reading for hours. The feel of trees, sky, earth, colour through his body, pores, tissues, cells. People in the park tended to look happier. Not always true: he saw the needy, the vagrant, the dangerous. But most people seemed happier in the park than outside it. He felt he might sleep there and be at peace, but went back to his place in the end, feeling the afterglow.

About eight or nine months out of hospital, Kurt took to going to films. If he liked a film a lot, if it gripped him, he might watch it all day and evening, show after show. I once had a man in therapy who recounted an incident in which he ripped the television out of its moorings to stop his young son from watching films hour after hour. Now, in therapy, so many years later, he felt he ripped something essential out of his son, a piece of his son's essence. He regretted many semi-violent things he did thinking he was setting boundaries, being a father. His son grew up to be a film director, so who can tell what led to what, whether the combination of intense, rich watching cut by loss was crucial or not. His son's best film was about madness and loss.

I had the thought that, for Kurt, watching films linked with fairy tales in childhood. A kind of creation or re-creation of being read to by parents at bedtime. Only this time there weren't real parents to mess up. "It's like being injected by life," Kurt once said. "I'm on life support. I'm on intravenous with the screen. Life-feeling feeding me through the people on the screen."

"Feeling going from them to me," was another way he put it. I thought of breast feeding, although what Kurt described was not a milk feed but a feeling feed. I suspect that a feeling feed is always part of a milk feed, whether nourishing or toxic (Eigen, 1999, 2004). One can point out that Kurt was receiving, not giving. He was not interacting with alive real others. He was deeply immersed in acting on the screen or, rather, it deeply spread through him. But alive give and take?

I know therapists who emphasize alive give and take and would be sceptical about tolerating seemingly autistic states for long. They would coax the person to interact, not to be alone so much. I cannot say what works for others and I am far from the same all the time. But I felt something healing in Kurt's walking, sitting in the park, reading, watching films. He called it an "infusion of life, spirit, feeling". Deeply passive nourishment, an "infusion of life".

Being with me was challenge enough, even though I did not go out of my way to be irritating. I am irritating enough just the way I am. The fact that Kurt kept showing up, talking, being with me, tolerating me and my quirks, utterances, silences, and brainstorms was plenty, perhaps all that he could take. It might be tempting to criticize what was not happening, but I felt it was good to support what was. Maybe I was just another film on the screen. If that was so, let it be a good one or, at least, a bad one that takes him somewhere.

A year and a half into therapy, he began working at coffee houses. He left his first jobs or was fired, but somehow settled into a café that struck his fancy. He did not have to start work before four in the afternoon, which gave him enough dawdle and do nothing time. He began to see that some people were regulars and looked forward to seeing them day to day, week to week. He really was not part of their lives or they his. But, in a way, they were a deeper part of his life than they could know. He fantasized about them and also about people who came and went. A bit as if they, too, functioned like actors on the screen, as infusions of life. Except they were real, live three-dimensional people. Of course, so were the actors on the screen. But in the café he had to offer something, give something of himself in three-dimensional reality with real live people in the here and now, people playing no part except being themselves. He had to take and bring orders. He had to give nourishment. And it was a secret pleasure to do so. I did not call attention to the fact that his world was growing. I did not rub his nose in his growth.

Winnicott (1988; Eigen, 2009) writes of a time when the quality of an infant's aloneness depends on the quality of support it receives. A care-taker can support or intrude upon peaceful alone states, for example, when an infant seems to be resting quietly or staring into infinite horizons. A good alone state depends on the sensitivity of the care-taker as background support the infant does not know it has. I call this kind of background presence an unknown boundless other.

Insensitive wounding of this needed aloneness can have long-standing consequences. Some people try to heal wounded aloneness by using drugs as boundless support. Paradoxically, both a solitary life and a compulsive inability to be alone may involve wounded aloneness. We defend against the pain of wounded aloneness or collapse through it, and in some cases, driven to extremes, become murderous or go mad.

As we grow, the aloneness that received nurturance supports us. A background aloneness, elusive and poignant, touches our beings. Part of what we do for each other, all through life, is to support the aloneness that informs and supports us.

I think one thing that Kurt tried to do, with at least partial success, was to constitute situations in which he could live or relive a better quality aloneness, an aloneness that was a kind of home base from which he could branch out. Once respecting it in oneself, one respects it in others as well. We have a mostly unconscious tuning fork that resonates from aloneness to aloneness. Much depends on the quality of this resonance, the quality of support one's deep aloneness received, the quality it is reaching for now. Once the aloneness at the heart of our beings is allowed to develop well enough, one draws sustenance from it all through life. The quality of aloneness has its own growth curve that keeps developing. In this we become, in part, our own midwives, but we need help in doing so.

Something in Kurt "knew" what he needed, a "feel" that led him to the parks, the rivers, the cinemas, the cafés. This was not a conscious plan, not willed. It happened. It grew spontaneously, step after step, without realizing steps were in process. In retrospect, we became aware that we lived through parts of larger processes, but at the time it felt like everything was up for grabs. As, perhaps, it always is.

Therapy played the role of unknown boundless other in its background support and presence. Unknown to the therapist as well. Inevitably, we lack faith, patience, and tolerance. But messing up is part of it, too. The background, boundless unknown works with mistakes, too. Messing up is a part of existence, perhaps a needed part. There are many threads in therapy. Along with support for aloneness goes a better, fuller recovery from injuries aloneness receives, ability to go through messes together in more generative ways than the toxic impasse that nearly destroyed Kurt.

When we had been a little over two years together, Kurt began taking boat rides up the Hudson River, stopping at scenic places for an afternoon, sometimes overnight, Bear Mountain, for example. He would hike, rent a canoe or rowing boat, and just be, no goal, no aim. He soaked up nourishment without pressure. A woman friend (Kate) he met at the café began to appear on these trips and another dimension of life began to open. No ties or promises, but two people who liked to be together, exploring what they could, what life allowed them to share. Kurt kept repeating a William Blake mantra, "He who kisses each joy as it flies, lives in Eternity's sunrise." The other part he was not too sure about, but stumbled, "He who binds to himself a joy, does the winged life destroy." He was practising keeping himself from destroying what was possible, no simple challenge. Kurt was living, or got a taste of living, a kind of beatific eternal now, heavenly moments, a vacation from hell. Dotted moments, sprinkled over time, but a reliable part of his life. One does not have to go outside of time to find eternity.

*   *   *

Five years into therapy

Kurt speaks of a dream he had during the week.

"I opened a door and walked down a corridor to a lit room, orange glow, floor littered with papers and books. It was an old apartment of mine I forgot about and hadn't been in for a long time. I felt I was discovering it for the first time, a place I never knew existed. Was I alone? Was someone else in the building? Had someone broken in? Was I in danger? I felt alone and cosy and warm, a pleasure in this place.

"I looked up and saw a spider or scorpion, a creature that was both. Instant terror. It was going to poison me, kill me. I kept looking at it and the thought came, 'It's my mind.' I felt a release. I saw through fear I had all my life. Fear I see in people everywhere, basic fear. I stare at the spider–scorpion and think, it's my own mind I fear. This poison, this fear of getting killed, the spider–scorpion—my mind made it up. I created my own paranoia. My mind creates it. I feel like weeping, laughing. Something is lifting. Breath is coming back."

Kurt stopped breathing when he saw the spider–scorpion. It was as if his whole life stopped breathing. Breathing stopped long ago and now began again. Of course, such a statement is a figure of speech, but not only a figure of speech. It touches real constriction and a moment of seeing through, a moment of opening. A moment that happens over and over, a basic rhythm, contraction—freedom.

In this case, a moment of freedom from himself, from paranoid mind. He had an instant in which he saw through emotional excess, hysteria. One moment, a magnified fear: he would be helplessly penetrated by spider–scorpion stings. The spider–scorpion structure takes many forms, stands for all things bad: remnants of parental poisons, school wounds, relationship scars, danger on the street, poisons in the culture, in therapy. All congealed into a packet he suddenly saw through. "I have no excuses now," he said. "I can't make believe I'm as frightened by everything I thought I was. I am less afraid of what I fear, less afraid of being afraid."

*   *   *

A week later he asked, "Was the bug in my mind real? Did I make it up? Did my mind make it up? Both real and a creation? Real terror. Bad things happen. Death happens. Illness. All this is real. My childhood happened. It was real. Yet mind rolls it up into fiction, pervasive fragments take you over. Mind is the bug. It all depends on how your mind takes things. It funnels experience through the spider–scorpion and you go crazy, hysterical. You accuse, smash, blame. Totally caught by a paranoid prism. Paranoia is real. Suspicion and horror is real. The ground opens up and swallows you every moment. The poison is always there, ready, no matter how carefully you walk. You are always in danger.

"But to see mind as dangerous, you can't go back from that. I saw it. I saw through my mind. I can't say I didn't. I may forget I did. I may act as if I didn't. But the truth from now on is: I did have this moment in a dream. Something in me awoke from the dream in the dream, a lucid moment where I saw that the danger was a figment of my imagination—even if it was real!"

I said, "It's awesome to see the mind work, the dream working."

The sands may cover this moment, this realization , and we may start from scratch again in a week or month. But what Kurt said of himself was true of me, too: we saw something we could not permanently undo. In speaking of his dream, he brought me to a place where we saw through mind together, the prison of mind. How good it felt to breathe!

*   *   *

Paranoia constricts breathing. Paranoid breathing. Do we have a paranoid mind? Is mind necessarily paranoid? Did Kurt find that mind is paranoid or that he was paranoid about his mind? He seemed to say both and I feel compelled to go along with him. Or, at least in some strong sense say that the world or a part of his world, his world in a certain profile, was (at times, sometimes long times, a lifetime thread/threat) reduced to a paranoid lens. In contrast, how clear and liberated he felt seeing through that lens, seeing the spider–scorpion threatening to drop from the ceiling on to him, into him, devastate him, and seeing that the spider–scorpion was something his mind made up, a mental image, an image of his mind or an aspect of it, a dream image. The paralysis of helplessness was real, but lifted in the puff of light.

Each time I go through this moment I get back to breathing. The spider–scorpion tightens the mind. Seeing through pops it, loosens it. Body returns, flesh returns, together with another sense or use of sensitivity. Not just sensitivity to poisons but the living, breathing body, *jouissance* of existence. Living through such moments brought me as much relief as they brought Kurt.

*   *   *

Still five years into therapy

Kurt weeping, head in hands. "I feel now the way I so often felt in hospitals. No, not so often. But in my hospital stays there came moments when I put my head against my arm, leaning against a wall, and wept and wept. Sobbed. I did not wail because I did not want to draw attention to myself, at least not so much attention that an attendant would rush over. I sobbed on the quiet side but was noticed anyway. An orderly would come and ask why I was crying, a reasonable enough question, of course. What could I say? I told the truth, although I feared the truth was incomprehensible.

"Now for the first time I will say it as I felt it. I tried with doctors but no one could listen it through. In my last stay, a hospital therapist interrupted me as I started to cry in her office. She asked what I was crying about and when I began to tell her she cut me short and wondered why I was feeling such things. She seemed to feel they were, well, not real enough, too metaphysical.

"I was crying for the world, the whole world, all time. All the time of humanity, since the beginning of human time on earth. I saw the floors and walls of the building as levels and sections of time, ages of man, from human origins through Paleolithic, Neolithic, ancient, modern, now . . . all ages, each in its own right yet also compressed together as one. Humankind as one, one time. The separation of then and now was real, each epoch real. The separation was artificial, all one. How can it be both? In experience it *is* both.

"I suppose in another mood I could have laughed with joy. But that is not what happened. I wept and could not stop weeping for all the pain in the universe, our universe, the universe of our lives, human life, all human lives. Maybe all feeling beings. Maybe the whole universe, in its way, is a feeling being. As a child, I felt rocks were alive. Rocks change colours, shapes, grow with time, permeable to the great forces of time. You wrote of your experience at Yosemite National Park in *Feeling Matters*. The great rocks were alive for you. All time is alive, one.

"But I was weeping over human pain. My pain, your pain, although I did not know you then. Pain everywhere—time has no boundaries. All pain is one. Isn't that the meaning of Jesus? He took all the pain in the world into himself. All the pain in the world condensed to a single point that was Jesus. Like an alchemist, he transformed that pain into Joy. All the pain in the universe went through an inner transformation through His being. My weeping emphasized the pain. Another moment might emphasize resurrection.

"A suffering unto life. Life unto life. Weeping comforted me. I felt wholeness, peace in my chest, my body, my psyche. My tormented self found a moment of peace through tears for Everyone.

"I've tried to say this before. This is the closest I can get."

It took more than five years for a moment to come when Kurt could share this with me. More than sharing, expressing something aching for expression, awaiting the moment when it might be possible to say and be heard. All the pain of his life, the life of the world, human pain acknowledged. It sounds trivial to say that pain finally got validated, no questions asked. The reality of pain was/is real. Yet, in Kurt's life—and in how many lives?—does this fail to happen or fail to happen well. How often does feeling pain and trying to express and share it become short-circuited? Something goes wrong in the telling or the listening, something aborts. How to sense and express and share and hear one's feeling being is a capacity that needs nourishment and acceptance in the larger culture, as well as in one's office. There is still, this moment, a taboo against feelings, as if there is dread we will not be able to function and meet society's demands if we feel what we feel, if we feel our own lives. What more can be said, need be said? Kurt and I were grateful that we managed to co-create space to say what was needed, space that took years to grow. To find this space takes hard work and grace.

*   *   *

Twelve years into therapy

"I'm thinking of a movie I made five years ago, my first. I started out to make a documentary about a homeless woman, a bereft soul lost on this planet. Gradually I shifted to ways she took care of herself, habits of cleanliness and care, attempts to enhance her life. Somewhere along the line I lost interest in details of her life and began picturing moments of beauty. We'd follow her along her route and tried to follow the line of her eyes, what she saw, and in addition to the filth and speed of passing events, people, cars, stores, gradations of wealth and poverty, our cameras became magnetized by unsuspected beauty. It could be a corner of a building, the colour of the sky, light on the pavement, grains and textures of stone or skin or cloth, a passing baby. The cameras breathed their own life and followed what they wished and brought me to points of amazement, over and over. The world she was in was awesome. Terrible, too, dangerous, threatening. But she did her best to find patterns of safety. And the camera found inexpressible beauty as she moved, as if the cameras were eyes, additional psychic eyes revealing something she may have felt. Did we add this beauty to her life or did we find it within it, through her?

"I no longer called this movie a documentary. It was part-documentary. It was docu-fantasy. What was hers, ours, the cameras? We cut it to fifteen minutes and it got some play in independent movie houses. I spoke after the show in some of them, Q & A they call it. I gave some talks in colleges. It bothered me that I could not stick with pure reality. I could not stop the pull towards beauty. I gave into it. I recognized this as a weakness, one I cannot overcome.

"There are artists who can stick with the bare brutality of being, drive the tragic home. I give in to pathos, beauty in the weeds. If I saw cow dung in a field, I'd marvel at its swirls and think of a whirling top standing very still, a spiral nebulae in the dirt and green, with flies as signs of life. I've seen films of the worst brutality in war, in accidents, murder, even in surgery. I've no right to be attracted to the Beautiful Everywhere, as if it were Reality that Eased the Pain, a substitute reality, a primal reality. I feel guilty for my weakness. It will make me less of an artist, a failure.

"But I can't help it. It's who I am. At least, who I am so far.

"In one scene she sat on a park bench eating a crumbly sandwich. In front of her was an amazing oak tree, twisted, somewhat pruned but extravagantly wild, the way well tended trees can be made to look almost symmetrical, a giant snowflake. A feat because all its parts were asymmetrical, growing every which way, like wild hair, contained by an unseen principle of beauty.

"I smelled or imagined I smelled urine and anal or vaginal odour. A pang of repulsion when I thought of contact with her intimate parts. At the same time, I felt how hard it was just being, how for a moment she seemed outside of pain, sitting in sunlight, My eyes followed her eyes to the tree. I tried to find just the spot she looked at. I saw a demon in the branches, a demon's face. The configuration of the branches made a demon's face. I wondered if the camera saw it, too.

"What could I do, run screaming? I might have wanted to at one time. I would have been transfixed, paralysed. I would have felt it was a real demon. I would have doubted it was real but could not be sure. It just might be real. It probably *was* real.

"I stared and stared. Was I trying to see through it, pierce it? Or just trying to see what would happen if I did not budge, if I waited. Maybe I was just trying to see. Trying to see what's there or—and this is difficult—you know, when you look at a sunset it keeps changing, or smoke, or clouds. You get attuned to small changes. You get shivers from small changes. One moment demon, one moment tree. One, another, both superimposed, fused, separate. I watched the image change and wondered what was real and they all were real.

"I looked back at the homeless woman sitting on the bench and realized I had forgotten about her. I looked for a demon in her face but did not find it. What I found was a hard life, lines, marks, little holes, just someone, her own self, Through layers of time and wear, I saw basic goodness. Through distortions, deformations—Basic Goodness. The old oak came to life and glistened with Basic Goodness. And I thought, this must be true of me, too. Through rot, scars, warps—a feeling of Truth. If only I could hold on to it or it could hold on to me. I knew I would forget it, but would I forget it entirely? Could I? If I could forget it entirely, I would die."

I listened, felt his journey, his sense of something deeply felt. At some point I added, somewhat gratuitously, "It sounds like you found your way through to the category of the human." I meant by that something to do with mercy, caring, the feel of lived life.

Next visit he continued. "You must be wondering why I recounted a moment that happened five years ago and why I waited till now to let you in on it. It's time, is all I can say. It's also time for me to stop awhile, if I can. Katie is pregnant. I'm working like crazy. It's time to move on."

One could think: leave therapy just when a baby is on the horizon? Won't Kurt need help in the transition to fatherhood, its burdens and pressures? What is the logic of telling the story of the homeless woman and the demons in the oak tree, the discovery of basic goodness, and leaving therapy? It was Kurt's way of saying something happened and that now he felt it time to do the job himself, the job of being his own midwife, midwife to his life. It was time to meet his life, to live it. He was moved by the horizon, in awe that he could have a home and give himself to creative struggle.

* * *

Kurt knew that he could come back if he needed me or seek help elsewhere if he wanted. I am rarely "sure" when someone should stay or leave, unless the person was in obvious trouble. Kurt reached a point in his forties when he felt that his life was beginning and that he wanted to fully give himself to it. He had a sense that he *could* give himself to it and wanted to try.

Did his work in therapy immunize him from breakdowns? In his case, I suspect it did. I would not go so far as to say he assimilated his psychosis, but something like that was in process. Perhaps it had to do with going through states that would have maimed him without help. Listening was one ingredient, one he mentioned many times. Apparently, we created a situation in which he felt heard, in which he could try to contact what was in him and say what was there. There were other elements as well.

I think an unspoken one had to do with my own love of psychic life. I was interested, if not too tired or distracted, in anything that came up. Whatever came out of him, an ear was there for it, if not immediately, then at some point. This love of psychic life is a kind of background cushion, a psychic "feel", an appreciation. Whatever he said, I could find in myself.

Related to this is a need for psyche-talk, psychic hunger of a sort. There is a kind of psyche-talk that can sound odd to everyday discourse. Psyche-talk opens universes that arouse suspicion and rejection by our normative self. Psyche-talk can sound weird, extravagant, crazy, but it has a deep logic and, I think, we have a deep need for it. A need that our culture's emphasis on functioning obscures. A need that if shut off, comes out in crazy happenings, in war, economic and military madness for one, bizarre fads and manias for another.

Kurt's interest in film connected inner with outer. What he contacted through his breakdowns became part of his life's work. Madness informed his art. But it was madness, if not tamed, then circulated. States that entered processes of psychic absorption, psychic circulation.

Is madness too strong a word? Would it be better to speak of alternate realities, other spaces, other concerns? We are psychological amphibians, water and land creatures. More, as ancients hint, earth, fire, water, air, all dimensions of experiencing. One of our great challenges is flow between worlds. Taoism speaks of a hinge, the capacity to go back and forth, to pass in and out of multiple realities, to value the plethora of capacities that constitute us.

Somehow Kurt stumbled on an atmosphere that valued the range and mixture of realities he lived and, in time, he was able to make use of it. Not everyone can, and not every patient and therapist combination is a good match. Perhaps we were just lucky, luck tinged with grace, grateful for the way our relationship and work evolved. Perhaps Kurt and I tapped each other's sense of something that Robertson Davies (1983, p. 235) describes as "some power unidentified but deeply felt".

CHAPTER SEVEN

Arm falling off

I n a passage in *Cogitations* (1994, p. 231), Bion reports a patient's
dream in which the dreamer's arm falls off when he tries to
signal the train he is on to stop. He fears the train is heading for
danger and puts his arm out the window to give the stop signal one
might give in a car. His arm falls off.

Bion tells us that "the patient was not responsible for driving the
train; he wanted to be helpful and warn the traffic against a possible accident due to ignorance of the train's movements" (*ibid.*). So,
it may not be the train personnel he was trying to warn, but pedes-
trian or car traffic. Or perhaps another train? Whatever disaster the
patient warns against, his medium of warning seems likely to fall
short.

This is a typical Bion vignette with its particular variations. A
"helpful" state of mind results in something bad happening. The
"bad" thing is sudden and unpredictable. In this case, one disaster
substitutes for another. An arm falling off is better than a tragic
train accident. He tries to avert danger at surprising loss to himself.

When I was a child, my parents would say, don't stick your head
(or hand) out of the car window, it'll get cut off, the castration threat
clear. Bion's patient's dream arm fell off by itself. No outside object

cut it off. An attempt to help and a destructive outcome conjoined, reminding me of the saying, no good deed goes unpunished.

But how "good" was this act? It seems a little delusional. To stop a train or oncoming traffic by sticking your arm out of the window and making a stop sign? Not likely to work. Why not pull the emergency cord? Not enough time, not convenient? If the patient was in a desperate state of mind and acted impulsively, it was not an act designed to get realistic results.

The road to hell is paved with good intentions. Such sayings highlight a link between help and destruction, tinged with a possible delusive element. We see parts of situations from particular perspectives. It is not unusual to act precipitously, misdiagnosing situations. Perhaps, in some sense, all action is precipitous, one-sided, subject to error, if not delusive. Yet one needs to act and, in this case, the individual tried to avoid an accident, but the means he chose led to unintended loss (for striking portrayals of attempts to help linked with destruction, read Phillip K. Dick's *Valis*).

Bion felt the arm falling off behaved spontaneously, impetuously not fitting in with the patient's will: "this, from his point of view, worthy behaviour did not meet with success because his arm behaved as if it were having a tantrum and fell onto the grass . . ." The arm had a mind of its own. It did not go along with a whim that could not work. It is not likely that one can stop a train or traffic by sticking one's arm out of the window. Perhaps doing so was an excuse to give the arm a chance to fall off.

From the viewpoint of the patient's "ego", the arm behaved badly, like a recalcitrant child who will not fit in with adult desire. There is something mean in human nature and something impish that will not fit in anywhere, a negativism that preserves some measure of autonomy. In growing up, there were stories and jokes about the penis having its own mind, subjecting one to embarrassment or worse. Cupid is depicted as impish, recalcitrant, shooting arrows with out of the box wisdom often associated with disaster. We speak of the blindness of desire, but desire often follows our eyes. Figures like Tiresias or the blind philosopher in Keats's "Lamia" show another kind of blindness, one that sees through snares and machinations of "des-ire". Worlds within worlds, words within words, each contributing its share to the colour, variety, and dilemmas of experiencing.

In the arm falling off dream, the recalcitrant arm may have accomplished the patient's purpose after all. Perhaps the train stopped in light of this situation, the rebellious arm causing a delay. At the least, the fall brought a pressing condition to the analyst's attention as well as the patient's. The patient intuited something catastrophic, a sense of disaster in process, a situation in need of help.

There are processes in us that sometimes bring intentions to fruition in exaggerated ways. Instead of a helpless arm signal, the arm falls off, upping the stakes. As if something inside knew the ordinary road traffic signal would be ineffectual and resorted to extreme measures. The will to foil and fulfil join, perhaps unable to tell the difference between success and defeat, since each has so many meanings and results.

We learn from another vignette how the meaning of a moving arm can be misjudged. "Help! Help! I'm drowning, not waving" (Bion, 1994, p. 231) Bion here expresses a state of catastrophe in process. Something awful has happened, is happening, will happen. Life and personality are marked by catastrophic processes, past, present, future—a prolonged SOS signal (Eigen, 1986, Chapter Three). The arm falling off dream begins by locating disaster in the near future—impending disaster. But the whole sequence may reflect something ongoing or repetitive, a sense of disaster that informs a person's life.

I mentioned earlier that Bion tells us "the patient was not responsible for driving the train" but tries to help, from his perspective, by warning against disaster. Here are a number of facets possibly linked with such a situation.

1. *Primal scene.* The potential train wreck represents parental intercourse and collision fears. The patient cannot stop his parents heading for disaster. Or pleasure. The association of fecundity and catastrophe runs deep, the joys and hardships of life, the pains of rivalry, inclusion–exclusion, exile–favouritism.

2. *Trauma.* Try as he may, the child can not stop the parents heading for disaster, whether fights, abandonment threats, or a chilling atmosphere of contempt. Neither can the child stop the parents from wounding him. He sees it coming and in

vain signals them to stop, wishes the bad thing will not happen again and again. At such a moment, the arm falling off signals helplessness. One cannot make things better. One cannot solve the problem of pain and injury. One cannot make the parents better or change their or one's nature. Here it comes again, another awful happening: "Please stop! Don't! Don't!"

3.   *Rigidity.* Is one responsible for what happens to one? We are told we must take responsibility for our lives, our trauma history. We must meet ourselves, struggle with our beings. There is something inflexible about a train. It perseveres on a track, something hard, strong, moving, containing, but monomanic, one-sided. A common saying: someone has a one-track mind. Sometimes this kind of perseverance helps, sometimes it is not very adaptive. Perhaps the train represents the patient's glimpse that there is something one-tracked, monomanic, rigid about him and that he wishes to change but does not know how. His attempt leaves something to be desired. Perhaps he senses links between rigidity and catastrophe but is at a loss. He feels he must do something to compensate for helplessness, but what he does causes other difficulties.

Bion stresses that the dreamer's arm acted independently. It did not subsume itself to the patient's presumed agency. The patient's project was to signal impending catastrophe, possibly with a hope that all would be well and he would be a hero and earn approval. Instead, a helping hand added to the difficulties of the trip and implicitly raised a general problem: can we develop less injurious ways of helping ourselves?

Bion brings out a link between helping and harming ourselves and others. In the arm falling off dream, the patient's attempt to help has unexpected consequences. He is at a loss as to how to approach or "solve" the problem of trauma, catastrophe, and helplessness. A certain blindness in human affairs is part of the implicit structure of situations. No one sees all facets of a situation (if there is such a thing as "all facets"). We are partly blind and often overestimate what we can see and do, an attitude that meets with surprises, as the dream suggests.

A bit of Babel

Bion uses several myths to help depict our situation: Eden, the flood, the Tower of Babel, and Narcissus. Each involves punishment for human activity and states of mind. God tends to be the carrier of the punishing force or tendency. Bion notes that individuals often cannot tell whether an emotion is inside or outside them, an individual may not recognize that "his own emotional experience appertains to himself and not his environment" (1994, p. 236). Since God is a character in our narrative, we stand to learn a lot about ourselves by examining God's personality (Eigen, 2002, pp. 140–148). Here we will touch parts of the Tower of Babel story as depicted by Bion (1994, p. 241).

The destruction of the tower links with the arm falling off or drowning (biblical flood, "Help! Help! I'm drowning."), a penumbra of associations involving emotional scattering and flooding. Bion speaks of the tower as "an artificial breast–penis", representing nourishing/fecund activity that binds people together. People gathered with high aspirations and willing labour, a communal effort to reach heaven, reach another plane of living by working together. God damaged this linking activity, as he wounded Adam and Eve for a nourishing aspiration (tree, tower, arm). There are many myths and stories about reaching too high. Punishment may come from outside or be intrinsic to the situation itself.

Some say Adam and Eve wounded themselves. Wounding processes are inherent in human nature. But we do reach—reach out, reach for, stretch a little more. Our implicit reaching urge was a possible factor in pushing our system towards an upright posture. Self-transcendence is a thread in our beings. A piece of the "fall" (the tree in Eden, the tower in Babel) may have to do with our reaching further and faster than our system can support. We get ahead of ourselves and lack resources to support our advances. Our means of production gets ahead of our ability to digest what we produce, whether the content is psychic, economic, or physical.

A theme Bion emphasizes in this story has to do with binding and scattering. He points out links between the binding activity of the word and communal activity of a group of people. Bion suggests that a word is a hypothesis that brings together groups of meanings. It unites under one rubric a host of possibilities, including opposites (opposites go together) which might otherwise be scattered. It sometimes seems mysterious how a single word takes on diverse meanings. It is a bit like geological layers and what they reveal about processes over time. Meanings are alive and spark unanticipated combinations, relations giving birth to new meanings, and all this may go on in a single word. Of course, words are not isolated, but occur in relation to other words, language flows, structures, intentions. But it adds to a sense of our condition to realize how much goes on in a single word, how much a word mediates and holds together.

By Bion pointing to God as carrier of unbinding, scattering forces, destroyer of links, he points to an autochthonous tendency inherent in our nature. Both binding and scattering play a role in creativity. The Tower of Babel story emphasizes destruction of creativity. God definitely seems mean and envious, attacking human co-operation, frustrating achievement, in analogy with the individual's dream arm falling. Some part of ourselves does not behave or co-operate. God here is an awesome prankster, perhaps with some parallel to a child breaking things just by doing what children do. To build, to destroy—tendencies that seem part of God, nature, ourselves.

We try to rationalize death and destruction as processes necessary for change. They create space for the new. How convincing do we find this? On a more subdued level, we readily see a multiplicity of processes in creative work and often speak of creating tensions in various mixtures of balance–imbalance. An artist may destroy forms that emerge, painting over them, layering, blotting out, until something more intriguing emerges. Today, critics like to speak of violence and violation in a brush stroke, in a gaze, as if accepting trespass and breakage as part of the movement of a work. Rock artists went through a stage in which they destroyed their instruments on stage, as if by breaking a source of their music they might go through the wall to the other side, beyond everything that can be heard or experienced—everything. A different venue than "spirit ditties of no tone" that Keats conveyed in his depiction of a Grecian urn.

How do we use materials to go beyond materials *vs.* how to use materials to bring the latter out more fully, subtly, unexpectedly? Both strategies reflect psychic urges, needs.

What Bion brings out in the arm falling off dream and Babel remarks is that a tendency to destroy our own products exists within us and has its due. Not only destroy products, but processes that produce them, linking and building activities. This destructive tendency may play a role in keeping things new. But there are ways in which it undercuts efforts, keeps us down, a kind of built-in Mafia ready to smash our knees just as we flex our powers. It may clear paths for the new, yet, also, make us fall, force us to be less than ourselves (masochism and the reversibility of success and failure), and sometimes force us to see ourselves, gain insight into ourselves, glimpse our psychic makeup. Bion brings us to the point of seeing that however destructive activity works at a given moment, it involves processes inherent to our makeup, inherent to our universe. It is ineradicable, but we may catch on to it a little and learn to work with it, mitigate and modulate it, even channel it. But first we have to see that it is here, inside and outside us, very real, and we do not escape it by trying to locate it only outside ourselves.

There are times when a destructive force tries to free us from existence, from the bonds of personality. When asked how to get to God, Plotinus replied, "Cut away everything." Jesus spoke of a sword to cut through attachment. An aeroplane pilot once spoke of having an essence inside that his personality covers and that destruction might free his essence. "I know I appear confident and competent, someone you could trust in the air. Everyone on the plane has their lives in my hands. I look the part. I know what I'm doing. Still, things can go wrong you can't control, you never know.

"But I can see when passengers look at me they respect me, they look to see if I'm the kind of person they are relieved to see. And most of the time that's exactly how I look. But inside I'm well, not just this calm, clear presence. My personality is like a shell around me. Inside there is an inner essence and how to tap that, how to communicate that I don't know. I'm trapped inside myself, better, trapped outside myself. I've grown around myself, so many layers of skin. But there is a deeper recognition I don't have a clue about.

"I love to fly. I'm free when I fly, a oneness of my essence and the heavens. Illusion maybe, but real when it happens. I look forward to that feeling. It makes me feel real. An illusion makes me real?

"There are moments I imagine bringing the plane down, letting it go with all its might, hurling towards the ground, smashing to smithereens. Everything gone. Sometimes I feel that's the only way I can rid myself of the shell. Get rid of all the cover all at once. I picture a full blown destruction that frees my inner essence."

A destruction that frees one's essence. Another variation of Eden, Babel, the arm falling off dream. Whatever role destruction has, it is a life partner. We had better find ways to get along with it, work with it.

The path of no path

Bion's examples suggest at least three modes or functions of destruction:

1.   A self-defeating mode. We undo, break down, destroy attempts to build, create, succeed. Most actions are composites, compromises between building and destroying tendencies.
2.   A chimerical tendency that refuses to get penned in, stultified. Something in our nature that eludes control.
3.   A nullifying tendency moving towards zero, void, nothing, unknowing.

Bion uses O as a symbol of unknowable ultimate reality. Milner (1987), when writing of Bion and mysticism, writes O as 0 (zero). A zero with many facets.

For "nihilistic" mystics and negative theology, a path towards God is, "Not this, not this." Jesus touches this when he says, "Forgive them, Father. They know not what they do." Change *they* to *us*: *we* do not know what we are doing. And, to a large extent, we do not seem to want to know or perhaps be able to know.

Bion, time and again, brings us to a point of radical unknowing, which for him is a constituent of the psychoanalytic attitude. To reach heaven by building a tower is an affirmation of knowing. To suffer defeat in this attempt is to experience a depth of inability, incapacity, unknowing. Unknowing has its own power, creativity, awe, its own transformative role in who we are, how we live, and how we feel to ourselves.

In one section, Bion distinguishes between a situation in which an emotional experience is secondary to the problem that needs to be solved and a situation in which the emotional experience is itself the problem (1994, pp. 234–235). In the former, the usual panoply of cognitive instruments may work. Processes such as analysis and synthesis may open possibilities and get somewhere. However, where emotional experience itself is the primary problem "there is probably no way of regarding the problem 'as' anything at all" (*ibid.*, p. 235).

A statement like that is a basic challenge to cognition, apprehension, understanding, and control. We are up against a problem for which means for achieving "solution" have not yet arrived, perhaps do not exist. It may be there are problems that have no solution.

I suspect Buddha regarded suffering as an emotional experience lacking a solution. No available discipline or method of cognition unlocked it. What did he do? He sat with the problem and sat with it. No way around it, no phoney solutions, no Job's comforters. He sat with the unknown. His method was unknowing. I propose that if one stays with a wall long enough—the proverbial banging one's head against a wall—something happens. The intensity of staying with the unsolvable emotional problem (i.e., suffering) opens other psychic areas.

To stay with something with all one's might can perforate the psyche, take one to another place, a kind of psychic wormhole where intensity blows the psyche open and other experiential possibilities appear. To suffer suffering may not end suffering, but one's experience of it changes. In Buddha's case, staying with suffering led to Nirvana and back again, samsara ↔ nirvana. *He* was changed by the experience. Suffering did not vanish but something happened that made a difference.

"Unsolvable" experience "makes demands on the individual's equipment of intelligence and personality" (*ibid.*) which can force unexpected paths to open. I think of the old words, "everything stays the same, nothing stays the same". We are mutating beings and unsolvable emotional experience is a mutating agent.

Once, when meditating on Bion's discussion of emotional experience as a primary or core problem, I realized, "I am an unsolvable emotional problem. Life, my life is." Who I am, what I am, where I am are facets of an emotional nexus in which the term "solution" may be misleading. The emotional problem that I am has no end in lived experience, no terminal point, no QED. It is a path, and, odd to say this of an insoluble "problem", an opening. The wall I am is an opening.

* * *

Bion speaks of a vast range of psychic phenomena "with no apparatus for their formulation" (1994, p. 314). He states that his own attempts at formulating them must be taken akin to dream thoughts, dreams, myths, no matter how sophisticated he may sound. He feels that processes involved in dreams and myths may help us work with emotional phenomena that otherwise elude apprehension.

He applies this sense of limitation and opening to psychoanalysis,

> supposing that there is a psychoanalytic domain with its own reality—unquestionable, constant, subject to change only in accordance with its own rules even if those rules are not known. These realities are 'intuitable' if the proper apparatus is available in the condition proper to its functioning. [*ibid.*, p. 315]

In certain circumstances, one can intuit emotional realities one does or cannot "understand". This supposes that intuition is in good working order and free "from memory, desire and understanding". Bion notes that intuition can be damaged by understanding. He depicts radical openness to unknown emotional reality as a permanent, continuous discipline, a path.

It may be that emotional realities are experienced as having "areas of disturbance, 'turbulence', 'opaque' areas contrasting with areas of 'pellucidity'" (*ibid.*). You can think of the sky above as having stormy and placid areas. It may be not much is felt about an emotion other than disturbance or peace. In time, configurations may form and one tries to describe a presence in more detail, bearing in mind that the accessible does not exhaust the inaccessible.

A patient was fervently explaining that there are people he knows, he one of them, his parents others, who do not change no matter how much work is done. This man has experiences accessible to him he could only dream about years before (perhaps more accurately, could not dream about years ago, possibilities he did not know existed). He has opened radically, yet also remains closed. He experiences areas of change together with areas that might be described as a psychically closed fist. The latter preoccupy him and, in his mental calculus, cancel the former. Yet, he would not be without the former, although the latter is unyielding. In the moment I am thinking of, he devalued life, therapy, his parents, especially himself because of failure to change, as if change mocked him, tantalizingly unattainable. The door was closed and he was on the wrong side of it.

I said something like, "Maybe change isn't the thing. The people you talk about, including yourself, had a lot of experiences." "Yes, we have," he said. At some point, he wept, feeling all he had gone through, the richness of it, even if in some way he could not feel the richness. He knew there was love in his life and valued the going throughness of experiencing. Therapy supported him in face of all he could not feel, yet all he went through.

For a moment, experiencing was released from judging. Terms such as growth and change can be persecutory. One judges oneself in terms of how much one changes, not how much one experiences. Change persecutes experience. In terms of the judgement, "Thou shalt change, get better, grow!", experiencing is not enough. One judges oneself lacking if change is insufficient. One fixates on lack, insufficiency, and devalues all one went through, the whole of one's life, the experience of having lived.

Appreciation–depreciation. In my patient's case, the latter counted more. Nothing counts because something is wrong in life, his life, him. Yet, he was with me, fighting to be with himself. This I take to be a foundation of faith, as in the story of Job, where there is no comfort, nothing to hold on to, nothing to have faith in. And yet . . .

Where is the arm falling off, the crumbling tower of Babel, the loss, mishap, catastrophe? It is his own being, his psyche wrenched from itself in free fall down endless pits. And yet, he put himself maximally into living moments whether or not the moment had a vacant stare. He gave it everything he had.

Another patient, also giving it all he had, agonized over his I. "I read somewhere in your work that the I sticks out like a sore thumb throbbing with pain. I felt that all my life. I try to make my I go away, but it's me trying to dissolve it. I as it, a disturbance. *I* am a disturbance. I get a feeling that if I can get rid of my I, I'd feel better, clear. Saints try to nullify their I. I remember a passage by Thomas Merton who asked Buddhist monks in India whether they extinguished the I and no one had. Maybe they felt the attempt was worth the effort.

"How do you get rid of sin, evil, whatever is biting you. Something bites and never lets up. Do you get stronger over time or give up, lose energy? The biting doesn't stop. Is this something that can be solved or just lived with? People speak of pain waking you up but it can do you in.

"Two days ago—a miracle, a lucky turn of the wheel. It was early morning. I could neither sleep nor get up. Just lay quietly breathing, listening to my breathing, feeling it. Crying inside. Feeling there will never be a bottom, nothing will be solved. For a moment—I can't say there was no I or whether there was or wasn't—but it stopped torturing me. Where was it? There was something like clear sky. No trace of this versus that. No fights over who got it right, who got what, no positions, beliefs. Just something like clear sky. Where was it? Behind my eyes? In front? Or is it that 'place' isn't what you thought, words don't find it.

"I go on debating myself. But inside I feel happy. The clear sky that is no place fades but doesn't disappear. There are trickles. Trickles of no place, placeless place? The word place doesn't work. 'Don't leave me,' I want to say. But being over-dramatic won't do. I may miss the shimmer. Here comes a tug of war again but the shimmer doesn't stop."

This patient speaks of disturbance and peace in the same field of experience, throbbing I pain, clear sky. Is it confusing because our categories are not big enough? For the moment, self-destruction fades, but one is not out of danger. A surprise attack can happen any time. The attack may be a call to oneself to notice something left out, or a refusal to be boxed into a system, whether the system is a belief, an organizing behaviour, a personality pattern, or an attitude. Or a pure need to destroy. There is, too, an imp in us that keeps things going. Traditionally, an imp with many faces (Cupid, Pan, demons, the evil inclination).

For the moment there is a happy opening, relief, more than relief. An unexpected taste of experience one might not have believed existed, if one did not experience it oneself.

My patient adds, "Sutras often say enlightenment is omniscient, Buddha possessed omniscience or areas of omniscience. The clearing moment I experienced—no omniscience. Just there. It solved nothing, no answers. Yet somehow it's a relief to live in an answerless place."

The arm falling off dream and the Babel episode have a certain drive, striving, anxiety. The Babel story hints at a certain elation, then smashed hopes. They represent moments of turbulence, catastrophe, catastrophe anxiety. My patient discovered an area of contentment. Contentment is an inadequate name. But so are words like peace or rest or relief, moments of freedom from the burden of self, the torment of self. A Sabbath part of the soul, perhaps. Yet, the word "clear" kept coming up. Clear space. It seemed to be a visual or semi-visual experience, hard to locate, but something to do with the eyes or behind the eyes, although not limited to them. Seeing a clear space. Clear has ear in it, probably an accident of language or spelling with psychic reverberations. As if something about hearing, inner hearing, is relevant for what we can see. Bion notes an experience in which disturbance and clearness are parts of the psychic field (above).

The combination, storm–clear, are constituent psychic ingredients which may oscillate or work simultaneously (Eigen, 2005). They have many cultural and individual reverberations. Bombings of cities alternating with all clear signals, storms and the electric calm afterwards, fights between couples and making up afterwards, rhythms in sex, emotional upheavals alternating with calm, excitement, and rest or quietude, samsara ↔ nirvana. There exists a certain fit or resonance between outer and inner realities, whatever differences and dislocations.

My patient gave a special value to a clear moment he unexpectedly experienced. It solved nothing, but changed how he felt about things. Not simply less pressure, hysteria, drive, and dread, more a thawing, appreciation, not exactly accepting, but acknowledging. Some of the weight of life momentarily lifted and an aftermath remained. The moment continues to have effects and there have been others.

The last two patients I wrote of were tortured by their own psyches, psychic reality. One because he could not feel his life, the other because his I throbbed with pain. Both were in pain. For the former, I think of the tin man in *The Wizard of Oz*, wishing he had a heart. Perhaps wishing he could feel his own broken heart and the broken heart of humanity, perhaps God's. Some kind of faith kept them going because they gave life all they had. Not just to get ahead or be winners, the top of anything. To give life all they had because that's what life was to them. You give it everything you can. Their arms fell off and Babels crashed millions of times. But they kept going, driven perhaps to crack through a shield around life, an icing over, the crashes and falls often leading the way. The Bible repeatedly speaks of a hard heart, a change of heart, getting a heart of flesh, a human heart. To experience the heart of life with all one's heart and soul and might. My patients were beamed into that trajectory, whatever failures or successes, moments of opening and loss.

CHAPTER EIGHT

Music and psychoanalysis

[Interview by Stephen Bloch and Paul Ashton for their book, *Music and Psyche: Contemporary Psychoanalytic Explorations,* Spring Journal Books]

S TEPHEN BLOCH (SB): Your writing seems so intrinsically musical. As others have commented, you write in a powerfully evocative manner, often from within a musical psyche rather than about it. Aner Govrin, for example, has reflected on the musicality of your writing (2007). Can you give us some thoughts on how you respond and feel yourself musically in the analytic encounter?

In *Toxic Nourishment* you wrote tellingly about disturbed patients reaching for something musical in the therapist. I have carried this quote in me for a long time. Perhaps you can take further what this musical core is. Where are you in the room musically? Does this refer to specific works, themes, or auditory images, or to a broad musical sensibility?

MICHAEL EIGEN (ME): I don't think I especially think of music or think I'm tuning in to something musical in sessions. Although sometimes I hum a tune or sounds come by themselves or I sing a bit of a lyric. Occasionally someone asks me to sing a lullaby, like a mother might her child, and I may do that, quietly, not knowing what will come out, a mixture of sound, word, hum. At such moments, I feel my chest quivering, resonating heart to heart, and bordering on tears. It is often a Jewish melody I make up, and the person I sing to weeps deeply, as if long waiting to be touched this way, scarcely believing that it's happening.

There is, too, the innate musicality of speaking–pausing, like notes and rests, intervals, rhythms, all that happens by itself, and there is much to be said for this kind of "dance". Since I was a jazz musician, improvisation is natural in sessions, and I can feel syncopated rhythms, jerks, and pushes, fast runs and *legato*. All this and more happens implicitly and rarely is centred in attention. I don't think one is unaware of these shifts and their musicality, but they are not usually focused on.

Music is in the skin, the feel of a moment. I have often been told that the tone of my voice touches someone inside, as if my soul is in my tone. Voice varies and sometimes is more musical than others. One goes through a lot of changes. The changes a baby goes through in a few hours would exhaust an adult—if an adult went through what a baby does he'd have to go to bed for a month to recover.

I mention these things but they and others like them are not my focus of the moment. I want to bring out something deeper, you mention a musical core. There *is* a musical core. Perhaps more than one. For example, the sound of a session. How the session or a person sounds. People have, so to speak, smells—psychic smells—and they have sounds. The word sound, too, also connects with how sound one is—the soundness of mind or body or judgement or intention—hinting that in primordial language, feeling sounds. A popular song speaks of the sound of silence. There are also the sounds of feelings.

But here I want to go further and touch a soundless sound. There is soul music, inner music, akin to the music of the spheres. You can hear it. Yet, it has no sound at all. Profoundly silent. Yet, this silence sounds. It is deeply musical. Keats writes of "spirit ditties of no tone". There are moments when this no tone is the inaudible tone of the universe. Poets often use words to communicate wordless realities. We speak of vibrating to one another, or a bell ringing inside, or my bell ringing your bell, or yours ringing mine. What is it that rings? You can hear it or almost hear it—by what sense? Does quiet have a sound? My quietness and yours— hush, listen. Often we are told in the Bible, listen, hear.

Hear, O Israel, be quiet, listen, and you will hear God. Not simply a still small voice or voice in the whirlwind, but the voiceless. The purest music that sets the heart aquiver, heart to heart. In some sense, perhaps, the music of the spheres was a "projection" of music of the heart. Heart-music pervading, informing human life. Why not? Why so much cacophony? I once heard a bell made in Ireland arouse a taste of this purity. Pure sound. A divine tone in the flesh, mediated by the ear, the ear–soul or ear–heart connection. The word heart has ear in it, hear. An intimacy between ear and tear, to be touched by what one hears, moved to tears. We have a very musical body, a very musical mind. Yet, there is music that hides this fact and music that shows it or is it. Voice, sound, impact, emanation. For Milner, places in the body were very important. Both Milner and Bion painted. Yes, painting is visual and an externalization of body elements as well. But it is also more and may come from body tonalities and give the latter expression via visual bodies. Some painting is musical. Kandinsky's, and perhaps Miro's, consciously so. In some way, if only at moments, we have a musical body.

Perhaps music is even a basic structure of our bodies, our rhythms, timing of processes. Perhaps there is a special ear that "hears" body times, rhythms, tonalities, and builds on them, with them, an inaudible kind of hearing that feeds sound.

sb: I am struck by how early in your response you have foregrounded silence and its place in music (or music's place in silence). I think of two contemporary composers, John Tavener and Arvo Part (the so-called holy minimalists) who deliberately use and relate to silence. A book of interviews with John Tavener is entitled *The Music of Silence* (1999). Arvo Part, in "Cantus in Memory of Benjamin Britten", begins the work with three "beats" of silence, bringing silence into the conscious awareness of the musicians and then the audience.

Your reflections on music and Bion's notion of alpha function are a particular area I would like to explore.

me: As mentioned near the end of my last response, music can show, music can hide. One can go further. Music can foster music or kill music. By that I mean, too, music can mediate psyche or kill psyche. We recoil at suicide but we are suicide prone beings. We all kill ourselves one or another way.

One thinks of the huge importance to USA veterans that soldiers missing in action had. After the Vietnam War, obsession with combatants missing in action mounted. In retrospect, part of this must have had to do with a deeper sense that soldiers who returned were also "missing in action". A recent movie, *Waltz With Bashir*, shows the blotting out of vast areas of self and experience in face of war horrors. A lesser-known recent movie, *Leave No Soldier*, also focuses on this theme. The human psyche has the capacity to blot itself out in order to survive. We have defences ranging from ignoring, numbing, deleting, dissociating, blotting out, killing off— killing off parts of ourselves or our capacities in order to go on living. Music plays a complex role in this, too, as the soundtracks for the above two movies show.

Much hinges on how we use our capacities and ourselves, how functions are used. They can be used in nourishing and/or destructive ways. The same capacity, for example thinking or feeling or imagining or acting, can be used to enrich or impoverish living, to add to life or add to deprivation. Emotional starvation and emotional over-eating are both real, depending, in part, on how emotions are used, how we relate to them, our modes of approach.

In the hands of the Nazis, music became an organ of the state, to incite, cajole, push people past natural inhibitions to the point of aiding atrocities on a massive scale. This kind of use of music is not unusual, although, in Nazi Germany, the scope and horror of its use reached new levels. Music helped people go past the horror barrier and do things that might otherwise repel them. This is not what I call alpha use of music, not music for psychic nourishment in the profound sense. Perhaps you might call it ersatz nourishment, but that is too weak. Mock nourishment, demonic nourishment? There is such a thing as feeding devils, and music can play a role. But alpha music?

What can I mean by alpha music? In a chapter called "A little psyche-music" in *The Sensitive Self*, I note that a ball player can make a great catch one moment and drop the ball the next. One moment, alpha body, the next a beta moment, one moment flowing, the next blocked, paralysed. Likewise dancing. One moment you move fluidly and freely, dancing is wonderful; the next you are all left feet and stumble over yourself or your partner. Alpha movement one moment, beta another. So with any activity or capacity. Jazz musicians speak of being in the zone and at other times it's cliché. Alpha one moment, loss of alpha another.

An important aspect of alpha function is the role it plays in emotional digestion. When music is musical and music-ing, when it is alpha-ing, it not only mediates, conveys, and stimulates emotion, it also plays a role in processing, digesting, creating it. It is an important quality of alpha music that digestion and creation go together, that creation is a form of digestion and vice versa. The same happens, say, in Rilke's poetry, where an alpha word opens reality, creates reality, and at the same time begins the digestion of its creative transformations.

SB   The idea of opening and digesting experience is a powerful way of understanding a helpful analytic interpretation.

ME: Jesus signalled something like this when one moment he praised his student, saying "he is with God", the next moment saying of the same disciple, "you're of the Devil". This is a matter of spirit, some say intention or, as I've sometimes called it, affective attitude. There are affective attitudes that act as feasible frames of reference and modes of approach to experience, which enrich the human spirit and life, mediate the creation and digestion of experience. And there are attitudes that poison experience. The Bible is always asking us to choose between sin and goodness, alternative paths of being. Perhaps what it is getting at, over-literally, also has to do with quality of feeling attitude, quality of heart–mind, or, in Bion language, quality of heart alpha, mind alpha. "Thou shalt know them by their fruits," says Jesus of prophets or, in this Bion moment, thou shalt know them by their alpha, by the way capacities are used.

SB: You are highlighting the fact that music can be destructive as well as constructive. This is an important caution against a too sentimental understanding of the relationship between music and psyche Some writers, in their enthusiasm, focus only on music's beneficial aspects. However, Gurdjieff, in writing about "objective music", stated: "There can be such music as would freeze water.

There can be such music as would kill a man instantaneously". I am obviously not concerned with any physical claims here—but the thought of music that can block emotional sensitivity ("freeze water") and deaden aliveness is powerful. This is obviously close to your concerns in *Psychic Deadness* and "Killers in dreams" (*Emotional Storm*).

ME: (That is a) wonderful quote.

Yes, it is said of God and Medusa that seeing either of them can kill you. It is a common saying, "I die, I die" when under the sway of deep feeling, erotic or sheer poetic, musical beauty.

One feels one will go under, under the impact of unbearable beauty.

It is also true that music can function as a toxin. But it is also true that its power or beauty can destroy your usual way of organizing experience, destroy your own cliché, or habitual style, a radical revision of the psyche just by hearing a few notes. I was destroyed by the beginning notes in Beethoven's 14th quartet and by a few sounds the first time as a very young man that I heard Bartok. My approach to sensitivity underwent radical reworking in an instant. What I was moments before no longer existed, except perhaps as a dull shell that would haunt me like a ghost, skin that can't ever quite be shed, but that was already dead, gone, old and buried. What the quartet and Bartok opened carried me into the me of the future—then!

SB: Would you share with us some of your thoughts on Freud and music.

ME: Everyone knows Freud said music wasn't his thing. His writing wasn't especially flowery, but there was a poetics to it, a deep music. The biggest award he got in his lifetime was a Goethe award for literature. There is deep music to his thought and his clinical theory has to do with listening, hearing. He is rightly famous not for discovering the Oedipus Complex, but for using the Oedipus story to aid in discovering psychoanalysis (as Bion points out). Too many of his followers soon enough used psychoanalysis to reduce the arts. But the deeper truth is that the arts opened and continue to open psychoanalysis.

In one of his later works, "Analysis terminable and interminable", there are two or three pages packed with musical possibility, suggesting an inherent rhythm of the psyche that can go
wrong. In condensed fashion he brings together a number of tropes
to evoke a sense of a stuck psyche, sticky or inert libido, something
resembling entropy, a loss of psychic energy (he notes that the
psyche has a fixed amount of energy, but via the death drive some
can be lost in a fashion that is not known). In one or another way,
loss or presence of vitality was a theme throughout his work from
the beginning, when he wrote of loss of energy, weak libido, neuras-
thenia. My chapter on Freud in *Psychic Deadness* goes over this in
detail and the chapter on Freud and Sade in *The Electrified Tightrope*
adds.

What I want to bring out here is his noting in "Analysis
terminable and interminable" that in the case of stuck libido something is off with the rhythm of the psyche. He speaks of timing,
rhythm as basic to psychic function and experience. To be sure, one
can make a case for the possibility, even likelihood, that he had
Fliess' male–female biorhythms in mind. But I suspect this does not
cover the ground, although it may play a sub-role. Freud is writing
about a certain rhythm gone wrong, stopped, blocked, a paralysis,
a loss of rhythm and flow and is doing so near the end of his life,
when his own rhythms are challenged by disease, loss, and the
desolation of war besetting Europe, European culture implod-
ing–exploding in hideous ways with more on the horizon. The
death drive formulation comes towards the end of his life and what
may have looked like the end of an era of European civilization.
Paradoxically, the Second World War led to a more united Europe
in certain ways, but the problem of destructive force or energy still
looms large in human life across the globe.

I am interested in Freud's referring to something malfunction-
ing in the rhythm and timing of the psyche when he speaks of death
drive, masochism, inert, sticky libido or a destructive force, essen-
tially a self-destructive force. Something off in the music of the
psyche. I feel with his cultural background, which includes ancient
Greek literature and philosophy, that he is quasi-consciously–
unconsciously also referring to the music of the spheres, which
earlier I described as a projection of music of the psyche. We
have a musical psyche, a rhythmic psyche. As world music and

breakthroughs in modern music show, there are rhythms we do not know. Some get revealed/created as we experiment, as we listen and play and work. The emphasis on arrhythmia extends the horizon of what rhythm can be, surprise becoming a studied art.

When Bion was in New York, the only paper by a once New York based analyst he referred to was Theodore Reik's paper on surprise. Bion felt surprise was a constitutive dimension of psychic unfolding, rhythms of unfolding. It seems resonant that physicists speak of infinite dimensions enfolded in one another, implicit rhythms of enfolding–unfolding, akin to Kabbalistic formulations of above in below, below in above (as above, so below; as below so above), intricate interweavings of psychospiritual functions with emergent (surprising) possibilities. No accident that one of Bion's last seminars explicitly viewed psychoanalysis as akin to art (the Paris Seminar, 1978).

The music of the psyche, the rhythm of the psyche, can be a rhythm of surprise, a rhythm that plays against and breaks rhythm, that opens new rhythmic possibilities. Thus, rhythm is not necessarily a homeostatic thing. There are rhythms that destroy homeostasis, break new experiential ground. There are really amazing jazz drummers today who never seem to play the same thing twice, even when they do. Something keeps varying in thrilling ways, sometimes tone or emphasis or texture, but often sequence and pulse of whatever the drums pull out of themselves. When I was younger, playing in college bands, my favourite time was the end of the job when our drummer would play for us with his hands, no sticks or brushes, back to the hands, such a soft touch he had, and the rhythms never stopped changing. I could weep listening, my whole body mesmerized, needy, wanting more and more. No matter how long he played, I never wanted him to stop. My sense now is this is what psychic processing is like, what alpha is like, an ever-changing rhythm the depths and scope of which we scarcely can imagine. It is part of emotional life that we can express or narrate or convey only a bit of what we feel. We do not know the whole of it. There is always some frustration built in. It is like swimming in the ocean. We can never take in the whole ocean all at once. But we do swim in part of it and the water we swim in, while not the whole ocean, is real water.

In my chapter, "A basic rhythm", in *The Sensitive Self*, I try to bring out rhythmic variations having to do with coming through destruction, and use Winnicott's "use of the object" formulation, passages from Henry Elkin's work, and a Bion passage having to do with being murdered and being all right. Coming through destruction, a basic theme and rhythm. So much derives from it, including versions of rebirth, renewal, a new heart, but also a new realism, seeing things as they are. There are no contradictions when it comes to human capacities. Our job is to learn if it is possible and how it is possible to live in such a way that our diverse capacities are mutually nourishing and that all together they nourish life.

Bion writes of common sense and by this he means many things. The senses may not work in tandem. They may tear each other apart. And agreed upon common sense between human groups may not work in tandem, but heighten destruction via alliances (banding together in order to destroy targets). Shakespeare describes alliances as a way to jockey for power and destroy "enemies" or "obstacles." Links to destroy other links. Sometimes Shakespeare's logic is so black (Lear, for example), that destruction has the final word, with the exception that the viewer suffers a kind of "renewal" at seeing a truth of the psyche, a fact of life. The coming through, comes not in the play where all is nullity, but in the viewer. One goes through the experience and comes back for more. When it comes to making contact with life through Shakespeare, one always comes back for more. The rhythm of coming through lives through those who undergo Lear and receive the transmission, and go on experiencing what Lear opens up.

Freud takes the music of the psyche forward by variations on the theme of life and death and death and deadness. One who is dying may find in the process how alive he is at the moment of truth, instants before the light goes out (as Tolstoi depicts in *The Death of Ivan Ilyich*). Death makes me more alive, stimulates new rhythmic possibilities.

Freud speaks of consciousness as a psychic sense organ, a sense organ of psychical qualities. Language, too, can be viewed as a sense organ when used expressively, evocatively, when the concern is giving voice to feeling, letting feeling speak. Sense is a packed word, spanning many levels, from traditional references to sensory experience, to sense as meaning, common sense and a certain "realism", and this amazing meaning Freud touches, consciousness itself as a kind of sense organ, a sensing of psychic qualities. We have a sense of psychic smell and taste, the taste and smell of experience. We smell and taste each other's psyches, psyche to psyche, like dogs smell assholes. We smell and taste each other's personalities. Follow your nose, we advise someone who needs to use intuition. We mean a psychospiritual sensing. We speak of animal sensing, as when we sense danger or safety, sense the possibility of nourishment, sense a good or bad day, sense a storm, sense a moment of peace. What is this sense organ? Why call it an organ? Organic? Spontaneous? Something intrinsic?

Music is part of this domain of sensing, a special sensing that invisibly permeates our bodies, becomes our bodies. Music is part of poetry and art, rhythm and timing and colour and sound. But something else too, ineffable, a sense or feel, a musical feel, a musical sense. As you bring out, the possibilities of what is musical changes with time, age, culture, history. To what extent does music follow history, to what extent does it lead history? Herbert Read wrote that image precedes verbal idea by about 200 years. And music? We certainly are aware of correlations between forms of music, architecture, writing, and politics of an age. And Spengler writes of souls of cultures. The role that music plays in creating the tone or even forms of culture—more can be done. Music as a sense organ, like an animal senses scents in the wind, only more so, more fully, bringing into being worlds of experience that otherwise would have been silent or not been born at all.

SB: I feel a basic rhythm in the image of the Black Sun. This is a symbol with multiple resonances. On the one hand it is an image of a "destructive force" in the psyche. Taking it further, if one thinks of blackness as a negating force, then the black is the force of nullity, evacuating and emptying out. The Black Sun, for me then, is a pulse between emptiness and form, absence and presence. In an auditory channel the earliest origins may be in the sound, *in utero*, of the mother's heartbeat, an oscillation between nullity, absence, and connection, presence.

ME: Coming through destruction, a basic rhythm. Yes, but we come through only partially. We are engaged in lifelong births and abortions. Our coming through is partial. When there is rebirth it is partial. Some rebirths seem total and change the direction of a life.

But lifelong work on oneself continues in light of the new revelation. Every birth on the psychospiritual plane is also a partial abortion. And work on oneself continues little by little, day by day (sufficient unto the day is the evil thereof). There is beatific experience, revelation, a change of the Archimedean point of soul or spirit. But there is endless mop up work, working with one's character and personality, struggles with barriers and toxins. Near the end of *Feeling Matters*, there is a chapter called "The annihilated self," wherein variations of annihilated aspects of personality are expressed. Rebirth is partial birth and partial abortion. In *Coming Through the Whirlwind*, I speak of rebirth as a basic structure or psychic movement and experience, but often, rebirth rhythms are aborted and one keeps trying to right it, whether realistically, demonically, varied mixtures. Look what hells rebirths have wreaked. Yet, it is a basic experience that uplifts the soul. One we need to learn how to work with, an essential movement or rhythm we need to partner and develop.

SB: I have a simple curiosity as to the music that has meant a lot to you. What is the music behind you?

ME: I was pretty much born into music. My mother played piano, my father fiddled. I started piano lessons pretty young and played my first recital when I was six. When I was maybe seven or possibly eight, a man came around to the Catskill hotel we were at one summer, put a hat on the ground, took out black parts, assembled them, started to play. Blew my brains out, no, my heart, tore my heart and lit me up. It was, you guessed, a clarinet and he played Yiddish music. It was the most exciting thing that happened to me since I saw stars in the night when I was a bit over two and died inside. I mean died of joy, amazement, happiness, love. I couldn't stop staring. They lit my heart up. Now, years later, I can look back and also say that part of what I felt was love that such things could be. I fell in love with the universe, a love that remains, although I know how horrible this world can be and is.

At about seven or eight I started clarinet lessons and studied piano and clarinet throughout childhood. My clarinet teacher would play a little after lessons and I would laugh and laugh. He threatened time and again to stop playing if I laughed. But I could not help it. It was one of my greatest pleasures, to hear the sounds he made and laugh and laugh, they tickled me so.

As teens approached I felt I wanted to play tenor sax. I think it was sex. The deep sound of the tenor, sensuous, sexy, full, heavenly. It didn't light me up like stars or the clarinet sound, but it was part of growing up for me, going with girls, playing in bands. I think in eighth grade I started my first band and we played at a "Y" dance and stunk. I never played in a band that stunk again. I bought my own tenor and played until I was good. Sort of the way I learned to ride a motorcycle years later. I somehow or other managed to get it where I lived and rode it all night, falls and all, and by morning I was a cyclist.

I played sax through high school and college and a bit after. I heard Bird, and saw Miles when he was just starting with Bird, then saw Miles as he developed all through, saw everybody I could in those days, listened, imitated, tried things. Bud Powell became my favorite piano player but I also loved Erroll Garner and for a time in college Dave Brubeck. I started playing piano more. One day the piano player was sick and didn't show up for a job and I sat in and, in time, that's what I ended up playing for the rest of the time I played, through mid-twenties. I was getting deep into psycho-analysis by then and it is a regret that I did not keep on playing, too. I plunged into psychoanalysis, hooked by psychic life, and never came out. When my kids were growing up, one played bass, the other drums, so I played piano with them. It was a thrill playing jazz with my kids.

As hinted earlier, when I was young I loved Bartok, Stravinsky, James Joyce (speaking of music!), Klee, Kandinsky, but also Bach and especially Vivaldi. Vivaldi lit me up for a time like the clarinet and stars once did, and I felt it was the most centred music I ever heard. My taste now is pretty old-fashioned. When I put on a CD it tends to be Bach (solo violin sonatas), Beethoven (late quartets, chamber groups), Hayden, Mozart, Handel (solo piano). I'll listen to and dig anything you play for me but when alone my taste would seem pretty conservative to you now. When I play piano, it's my version of jazz. I say my version because I fear I don't know any better. Now and then my son the bass player plays with me and he's played with some really good pianists and I am grateful he tolerates me. There's nothing like hearing a bass when you play.

When I write I see colours and hear music, or maybe I should say hear the words musically, as colour and sound. I think I may have been in my early thirties when I dreamt that I should paint small, not large canvasses. You could see the canvasses in the dream. I took this to mean I needed to pour my creativeness into smaller frames, smaller work, and my first psychoanalytic writing involved shortish papers. I also published a short story and some poems. The idea that I was to do smallish things was freeing, took a lot of pressure off. I could compress a lot into small spaces. This led to writing being less fragmenting, depressing, injurious. I could write in small doses and condense the intensity and this enabled me to survive the process better in the long run. It takes a lot to learn what might work for one. In time, I found as a therapist that dosing things out was a key, at least for me.

The other day when I was thinking of words and wordlessness, the following came, two little bits:

> words as waves and wind
> ear to them
> listening to words as
> a sea shell
>
> * * *
>
> hearing sea
> in the silence
> of words

PAUL ASHTON: I had heard about the film *Into Great Silence* two years before it came to SA and expected that I would love it. When I finally saw it I had just come back from a two-week winter safari with my wife and daughter. We had lived close to the "ground" and experienced storms, floods, cold; wide, wide spaces, towering mountains, and an ever-changing night- and day-time sky. When I did see the film, apart from the long held shots of simple objects, suggesting mindfulness, I found it lacking. I wondered if this had something to do with the fact that we had experienced "God's Cathedral" and the film was about "man's monastery". The silence imposed on the monks is very different from the silence of the cosmos, which evokes something like "the absence of God in God's presence". Would you comment on this?

ME: Our experiences, Paul's and mine, are very different. I loved *Into Great Silence*. I had an immediate sense of recognition. The movie touched something in my spiritual core and had the effect of diminishing shame. When I saw the faces in prayer and meditation, I felt shells of shame begin to fall off my soul and inner body. Their faces were the way I felt and seeing them gave a kind of permission to live that part of me more fully, less apologetically, less defensively.

In our society, to be a man was to be aggressive, achieving, out for power, sex, money. Yet these faces, these supplicants—unashamed of the deep intimacy with God they touched and courted. To court God in deepest intimacy. Supplicants—a word resonating with supple. Instead of harsh, to be Supple. To unabashedly spend time with Intimate Presence, as much time as one wants or can. It helped free me to meditate and pray for longer periods, following the moment, on my knees, standing, sitting, head in hands, hands uplifted, head bowed, head lifted, heartfelt, ordinary, bored, caring. Whatever. It is a wonderful thing to give oneself this time, this contact with the Deep One. Perhaps at my age and condition time is more precious and the need for the Deepest of All is pressing.

I needed the faces of these monks but didn't know it. As soon as I saw them, I knew my own face, my inner face. I'm far from being psychologically blind, so I know the monks have problems, serious problems, perhaps with no way to address them. I take for granted we are all quite mad and wounded and have ways that work and others that fail to address our beings. For me, all this goes into parentheses. I do not need to know their bag of worms. I know what worms are like. What the faces of the monks who allowed themselves to be photographed gave me is what I needed this moment of my existence, permission to come out of closets I didn't quite know I was in, spiritual closets. To come out in the open—again, in new ways.

There is a silence deeper than music. Perhaps not even music goes all the way. Music can distract from this silence. There are times listening to music or playing it brings me deeper into contact with deepest silence. There are times it is an imposition, takes me away from it. It takes time and experience to be able to link up with how you feel from moment to moment. When to stop playing or listening, when to turn the CD off, when to fall on your knees or stand in hushed attention listening to—

Zen has an image of cutting a thread that holds everything. You cut this thread and words like stillness, silence don't come close. Some call it absolute Samadhi. It is breathtaking. But words like this are silly. As Zennists say, you have to experience it and experience it your way. When you know your Samadhi, no one can talk you out of it. You impose nothing on others or yourself. And when you come back you say thank you. Bow. Care. Life is in full bloom.

The deepest processing goes on in this silence. I don't know whether or not it is musical or music reaches it. More likely, music grows from it.

Music that grows from it and mediates it processes deep emotion as part of its work. To process feeling is one of the great tasks facing us as evolving beings. As one of my book titles says, *Feeling Matters*. Our ability to produce states is way ahead of our ability to process them. Music creates experience but also plays a role in processing experience. As other creative arts do, too. Dance creates experience and catalyses body processing of it at the same time. One might say dance is part of music or music grows out of dance or is dance. We can argue about primacies for the rest of our existence, which might be fun. There are networks of possibilities creativity opens. We do not know the beginnings or ends of these networks, which keep growing.

Any moment of art can take us closer or farther, open or act as barrier to the Deep Silence that prayer and meditation mediate. As mentioned above, Keats has a phrase, "spirit ditties of no tone". Yet, it is not simply this Deep Silence that we are after. We love the colour of sound. It opens us, soothes, excites, dumbfounds, thrills, nourishes. It can express catastrophe, faith, horror, foreboding and presentiment in instants. Silence and the colour of sound further each other, extend nuances and possibilities of both. They can, too, compete with and deform each other. So much depends on encompassing attitudes, implicit affective frames that are part of the background of creative work.

The night before I was to be on a panel discussing *Into Great Silence*, the following words came to me. Don't expect too much from them, just a little sharing of a passing moment.

They came after an hour or so of sitting quietly.

weight lifts, oppression lifts
heaven, hell and purgatory lift
beyond distinction and no distinction
beyond self and God.
great is Your faith
to live in Your faith

The words grew out of sitting for an hour, but refer to a Hebrew prayer said upon awakening. The prayer, loosely translated, goes something like: Thank You for restoring my soul, Presence in all, great is Your faith. At first glance, it might sound odd to praise God for His faith. Isn't my faith what's at risk? Then I realize, perhaps this means God has enough faith in me to give me another day. Another chance to make something of the time I have, to move someone, light someone, bring life to another place. God has enough faith that I might come through, worms and all. A communication one wants to share. The phrase to live in Your faith may touch another line from the morning prayers, "In Your light do we see light". The variation my words produced: in Your faith do we live faith. This faith is deeply musical. It is such deep music that it takes us beyond music, if that is possible

In *The Psychoanalytic Mystic*, I write that psychoanalysis is a form of prayer. Music can be, too. This does not mean prayer is all that psychoanalysis or music is. Far from it. But the link is worth entering. In my own life, they (music and prayer, psychoanalysis came later) grew together. I could fantasize that they have roots in my mother's musical voice when I was a baby. But then I would have to say, that her musical voice had roots in—love.

REFERENCES

Balint, M. (1968). *The Basic Fault*. London: Tavistock.

Bion, W. R. (1965). *Transformations*. London: Karnac, 1984.

Bion, W. R. (1970). *Attention and Interpretation*. London: Karnac, 1997.

Bion, W. R. (1991). *A Memoir of the Future*. London: Karnac, 2004.

Bion, W. R. (1994). *Cogitations*. London: Karnac.

Bohm, D. (1996). *Wholeness and the Implicate Order*. London: Routledge.

Bohm, D. (2004). *On Creativity*. London: Routledge.

Cleary, T., & Cleary, J. C. (2005). *The Blue Cliff Record*. Boston: Shambhala.

Davies, R. (1983). *The Deptford Trilogy: Fifth Business*. New York: Penguin Books.

Eigen, M. (1973). Abstinence and the schizoid ego. *International Journal of the Psychoanalytic Association, 54*: 393–397. Collected in *The Electrified Tightrope* (1993). London: Karnac, 2004.

Eigen, M. (1977). *On Not Being Able to Paint*. Marion Milner. New York: International Universities Press, 1973 (paperback). 184 pp., 49 illustrations. *Psychoanalytic Review, 64*: 312–315.

Eigen, M. (1981). The area of faith in Winnicott, Lacan, and Bion. *International Journal of the Psychoanalytic Association, 62*: 413–433. Collected in *The Electrified Tightrope*.

Eigen, M. (1986). *The Psychotic Core*. London: Karnac, 2004.

Eigen, M. (1992). *Coming Through the Whirlwind*. Wilmette, IL: Chiron.

Eigen, M. (1993). *The Electrified Tightrope*, A. Phillips (Ed.). London: Karnac, 2004.

Eigen, M. (1995). *Reshaping the Self: Reflections on Renewal Through Therapy*. Madison, CT: Psychosocial Press (International Universities Press).

Eigen, M. (1996). *Psychic Deadness*. London: Karnac, 2004.

Eigen, M. (1998). *The Psychoanalytic Mystic*. London: Free Association Books.

Eigen, M. (1999). *Toxic Nourishment*. London: Karnac.

Eigen, M. (2002). *Rage*. Middletown, CT: Wesleyan University Press.

Eigen, M. (2004). *The Sensitive Self*. Middletown, CT: Wesleyan University Press.

Eigen, M. (2005). *Emotional Storm*. Middletown, CT: Wesleyan University Press.

Eigen, M. (2006). *Lust*. Middletown, CT: Wesleyan University Press.

Eigen, M. (2007a). *Feeling Matters*. London: Karnac.

Eigen, M. (2007b). Incommunicado core and boundless supporting unknown. *European Journal of Psychotherapy & Counselling*, 9: 415–422.

Eigen, M. (2008). Primary aloneness. *Psychoanalytic Perspectives*, 5(2).

Eigen, M. (2009). *Flames from the Unconscious: Trauma, Madness and Faith*. London: Karnac.

Eigen, M. (forthcoming). Distinction–union structure, to be published in *Psychoanalytic Inquiry*, 32(2) (in press).

Eigen, M., & Govrin, A. (2007). *Conversations With Michael Eigen*. London: Karnac.

Fliess, R. (1971). *Symbols, Dreams and Psychosis*. Madison, CT: International Universities Press.

Freud, S. (1900a). *The Interpretation of Dreams*. S.E., 4–5. London: Hogarth.

Ghiselin, B. (1952). *Creative Process: Reflections on the Invention in the Arts and Sciences*. Berkeley, CA: University of California Press.

Goddard, D. (1932). *A Buddhist Bible*. Forgotten Books (www.forgotten-books.org), 2007.

Govrin, A. (2007). The area of faith between Eigen and his readers. *Quadrant: Journal of the CG Jung Foundation for Analytical Psychology*, 37(1): 9–27.

Grotstein, J. S. (2000). *Who Is the Dreamer Who Dreams the Dream? A Study of Psychic Presences*. London: The Analytic Press.

Grotstein, J. S. (2007). *A Beam of Intense Darkness: Wilfred Bion's Legacy to Psychoanalysis*. London: Karnac.

Humphrey, G. (1948). *Thinking: An Introduction to Its Experimental Psychology*. London: Methuen.

Levinas, E. (2000). *Alterity and Transcendence*, M. B. Smith (Trans.). New York: Columbia University Press.

Matte-Blanco, I. (1975). *The Unconscious as Infinite Sets*. London: Karnac, 1980.

Matte-Blanco, I. (1988). *Thinking, Feeling, and Being*. London: Routledge.

Milner, M. (1957). *On Not Being Able to Paint*. Madison, CT: International Universities Press.

Milner, M. (1987). *The Suppressed Madness of Sane Men: Forty-four Years of Exploring Psychoanalysis*. London: Routledge.

Mitchell, S. (1992). *The Book of Job*. New York: Harper Perennial.

Read, H. (1957). *Icon and Idea: The Function of Art in the Development of Human Consciousness*. Cambridge: Harvard University Press.

Sekida, K. (2005). *Two Zen Classics: The Gateless Gate and The Blue Cliff Records*. Boston: Shambhala.

Tavener, J. (1999). *The Music of Silence*, B. Keeble (Ed.). London: Faber and Faber.

Winnicott, D. W. (1969). The use of the object and relating through identification. *International Journal of the Psychoanalytic Association*, 50: 711–716.

Winnicott, D. W. (1988). *Human Nature*. New York: Shocken Books.

Winnicott, D. W. (1992). *Psychoanalytic Explorations*. Cambridge, MA: Harvard University Press.

INDEX